Politics in Education

THE LIBRARY OF EDUCATION

A Project of The Center for Applied Research in Education, Inc.

G. R. Gottschalk, Director

Categories of Coverage

I	II	III
Curriculum and Teaching	Administration, Organization, and Finance	Psychology for Educators
IV	**V**	**VI**
History, Philosophy, and Social Foundations	Professional Skills	Educational Institutions

Politics in Education

LAURENCE IANNACCONE

Professor of Education
New York University

The Center for Applied Research in Education, Inc.
New York

LIBRARY OF CONGRESS
CATALOG CARD NO.: 67-28052

PRINTED IN THE UNITED STATES OF AMERICA

Foreword

This is a bold and saucy book—outrageously indifferent to pleasing all of its readers all of the time. It dares to challenge our tribal lore about politics and education. Its tersely written chapters bristle with ideas and interpretation which, while always closely reasoned and often empirically derived, seem almost deliberately intended to confront aspects of the tribal faith. The author, Laurence Iannaccone, is, at one and the same time, a careful and wholly serious scholar and an irrepressibly gleeful destroyer of myths. And in the world of politics and education there is much magic to be exposed.

This is a large book—its brief 120 pages to the contrary. It attempts no less than charting the entire domain of politics and public education. And much more, it seeks to conceive of its field in theoretical as opposed to merely descriptive terms. The initial chapter uses general social systems theory to develop a model for examining political acts in education. One chapter on state politics utilizes post factum analyses of recent atheoretical studies to engender four generalized patterns which effectively categorize the political activities of educationists at the state level. Another chapter, again juxtapositioning data collected by others against the theoretical position developed earlier, sketches probable modes and directions of change in state education politics. In similar style the section on local politics reports, not isolated descriptive studies, but an integrated series of investigations developed against a common theoretical backdrop.

This is, indeed, an even larger book than the large world of education and politics with which it deals. In developing and illustrating the central theme, Professor Iannaccone crisply comments upon a rich variety of related issues; politics is, after all, involved in every educational matter. There is in the chapter on "Politics Preferred by Pedagogues," for example, a quick resume of the power struggles within the NEA. There is also an analysis of the discontinuity between contemporary educational problems in the public schools and bureaucratic structures established in earlier periods to meet no longer existing needs. The Board of Examiners of New York City is presented as a particularly dysfunctional agency. Throughout the volume there are incidental references to events and personalities—from Paul Mort to J. B. Conant to Everett Keith—which provide newer frames of reference for understanding our professional past.

In seeking to develop viable theory and to generate hypotheses about exceedingly complex matters, Professor Iannaccone demonstrates a laudable if infrequently observed courage in the academic world. It would have been far safer and far more natural to the tepid professorial temperament to attempt much less and to disclaim much more. He has deliberately, to use a notion he has frequently applied to administrators, maneuvered himself into a position of vulnerability. Many of his ideas, particularly in their details, will be attacked. Some aspects of his developmental construct will probably require restructuring. The conceptual leaps of much of his post factum analyses were admittedly made from precariously grounded springboards.

But what is essentially to be applauded is not Professor Iannaccone's courage but his considerable success. In my judgment *Politics in Education* promises to be a seminal volume for the field. I guarantee the reader will find it provocative. If you are occasionally indignant or even outraged, I'd suggest due caution before attempting to demolish his assertions. Behind his disarmingly impish style and his seemingly irresponsible hyperbole and over-generalization, there is, characteristically, considerable hard data and tough-minded analysis.

ROBERT SCHAEFER

Dean
Teachers College
Columbia University

Politics in Education

Laurence Iannaccone

A great many people, probably most people, have a rather naive view of education. They see it as a simple interaction between a teacher and a classroom full of pupils. Professor Laurence Iannaccone is, fortunately, not such a person. He sees and understands education as a major social institution subject to all the forces present in our society. He has been particularly interested in the way in which education has been shaped by political forces. Professor Iannaccone is one of the few who has undertaken the systematic study of the subject. This book is a progress report on significant findings of his program of research.

Professor Iannaccone's strength lies in the fact that he not only describes the political scene vis-à-vis education precisely, but he devises concepts which help the student of politics to understand what has been described. Further, he combines these concepts in such a way as to enable the student to predict the outcome of a series of political events. Thus, Professor Iannaccone fills the role of a social theorist par excellence. This book is full of theorizing of the type that is highly fruitful for education.

Professor Iannaccone studied political science at the Universities of Buffalo and Florence, earned his doctorate at Teachers College, Columbia University, and taught at Washington University, St. Louis and the Claremont Graduate School. He is (in 1967–68) on leave from his professorship in the School of Education, New York University. He holds one of the first post-doctoral fellowships in education given by the U.S. Office of Education.

The Library of Education is pleased to present this volume to the education profession. It should enable the profession to understand one of its most significant facets: the way in which political forces have shaped the schools of the land.

DANIEL E. GRIFFITHS
Content Editor

Contents

CHAPTER I

Politics and Education 1

An Operational Definition 4
Special Governmental Arrangements 8
Special Political Arrangements 10
Systems: General and Political 12
Dimensions: Governmental and Social 14

CHAPTER II

Politics Preferred by Pedagogues 19

The National Education Association 19
The Urban School 25
School District Reorganization 29

CHAPTER III

State Politics of Education 37

Legislation and Lobby 38
Typology: Four Linkage Structures 42
Correlates of Structural Types 50
Summary 62

CHAPTER IV

The Changing State Politics of Education 64

The Dominant Pattern 64
Changes in Types of Structure 70
The Developmental Construct 73

CHAPTER V

Change and Local District Politics 82

The Theoretical Backdrop 83
The Claremont Studies 89

CHAPTER VI

The Future 99

New Forces 101
Predictions 105

Bibliography 109

Index 111

Politics in Education

CHAPTER 1

Politics and Education

Politics and political activity are the substances with which this book is concerned. In an attempt to strip away vestiges of myths that perpetuate an artificial separation of education from politics, the author will confront the mainstream of American society where politics and education are actually enmeshed. The reality of politics will be explored through case studies on the local and state levels, and the word "politics" will be examined. A number of questions will be raised as guidelines, as points of departure, or as fuel for discussion.

What is politics? Trying to distinguish between political activities and other human activities, the scholar faces overwhelming difficulties. In the field of political science, where one might logically turn for definition, the authorities have not agreed on what the term "politics" means. Thomas Jenkin said, "It is a truism that wherever he is found man exists in a political society of some sort. . . . And yet the simple question of what constitutes political relationships and institutions has received no single, dependable definition." [1] If man does exist in a political society, then a pilot who has the task of defining "politics" must steer a risky course between the vast stretches that include all the rich variation of human social life and the scattered islands that select from the richness only a few elements which may lose their meaning in isolation. The venture of supplying a meaningful, universal definition can be left to others. The course here will be focused. By deliberately wearing blinders and thereby losing much peripheral vision, one can gain some incisive central vision. The price seems worth paying in this instance. A definition of politics can be used here that is less universal, if more limited, than would be necessary for a discussion of events or problems outside the governing of education in the United States. It is *the governing of education* which is the universe of discourse for this monograph.

Jenkin pointed out, "There are certain concepts, however, that have been uniformly associated with the idea of politics," [2] which suggests that the concept "politics" is a second order concept. It does not refer to a single particular identifiable aspect of observable phenomena; instead it refers to a cluster of concepts for particular identifiable aspects of observable

[1] Thomas P. Jenkin, *The Study of Political Theory* (New York: Random House, Inc., 1955), p. 4.
[2] Jenkin, pp. 4–5.

phenomena. Even the conceptual elements which Jenkin has cited as components of the concept "politics" are in the nature of complex abstractions. For example, he cited the concept of the state as uniformly associated with politics. In turn, the concept of jurisdiction over population and territory is "part of the phenomena summed up in the word *political*." [3] We are concerned with the idea of jurisdiction or governing over education, and we will be involved in two territorial units of jurisdiction in the United States—the state and the local school district—not because the federal level is without interest or importance, but because, until yesterday at least, the governing of education has largely been a state and local affair and this is where the reported data are. Thus, some of the difficulties presented to the political theorists may be avoided by sharply limiting ourselves empirically, taking into account the two universes on which the bulk of the data for the study of the politics of education exists.

The author has been largely influenced by recent research in the politics of education at the state level. This research falls into two categories: (1) research published in the last several years describing the politics of education in eleven states, and (2) even more recent unpublished studies of the politics of education in California.

A smaller portion of this writing is concerned with the local district level and, in particular, with the political processes of changing power and educational leadership there. Although not displaying as great a variation as two nation states, the government levels involved are quite different governmental and political universes. As a consequence, the concepts used in connection with the state, however adequate they may be for understanding the *state* politics of education, will not be adequate for the analyses of local governmental units or the national level, let alone for other countries and times. Thus, generalizations using such concepts will be confined to states.[4] In addition, the state level of this discussion will be largely confined to educational legislation in these dozen states. It will not be concerned with other kinds of legislation, nor with administrative or other agencies of government, except as necessary to carry out the central task.

Finally, the book will be more concerned with the activity of individuals, groups, and associations which influence or seek to influence the activities of legislators and legislatures in their decision making with regard to educational matters (it will be less concerned with the total activity of legislators and legislatures themselves) because here, focused upon legislatures, is the bulk of available research. To anticipate a bit, the nature of pedagogical politics—its sacred nineteenth century flavor in particular—makes legisla-

---

[3] Jenkin, p. 5. (Author's italics.)

[4] Obviously our concern with these states will be quite different from the political theorist's concern with *the* state.

tion central to any consideration of the state politics of education. It is probable, however, that the new federal interest in education will not only result in shifting the center of political gravity toward the national government, but will also reshuffle the historic relations among the state constitutional partners in policy making with respect to education, particularly the executive, the state boards, and the legislatures.

To be more definitional, by the "state politics of pedagogics" the author refers to those activities of educationists—individual, group, and associational—which are intended to influence educational legislation or which have a demonstrable consequence upon the course of educational legislation. In order to give an adequate description of the politics of educationists, an account of the activities of other individuals, groups, associations and, in particular, the legislature itself, will need to be considered from time to time. Other conditions, such as those produced by broad social forces, will not be neglected.

The final chapters of this book will be concerned with the politics of education in the local school district. Recently, many critics have stressed the "myth" aspect of local control as a useful correction to the view which schoolmen have often overstated. These range from James Conant to Nicholas Master *et al.*[5] and include the author.[6] However valuable it may be to point out that local control of education is inefficient or incomplete, it is not accurate to say that local school districts cannot or have not been able to *reflect the local citizen's will with regard to his school district.* Whatever the cogency of Mr. Conant's assertion that the prevailing pattern governing education, i.e., a state function locally controlled, has not dealt acceptably with segregation and the parochial school issues, the fact is that local school districts do display a capacity to reflect changes in the wishes of local citizens with respect to education. Local school districts which have been studied carefully have demonstrated a capacity to change educational policy makers and administration by means of the political machinery available to voters. Whether one likes what voters decide or not, what local district voters consider important enough to act upon is another question. In any case, the last portion of this discussion focuses upon the political processes characteristic of local districts when voters, exercising their franchise, change the system.

---

[5] James B. Conant, *Shaping Educational Policy* (New York: McGraw-Hill Book Company, 1964); Nicholas A. Masters *et al., State Politics and the Public Schools* (New York: Alfred A. Knopf, Inc., 1964), p. 6.

[6] Laurence Iannaccone, "The Future of State Politics in Education," in Frank W. Lutz and Joseph J. Azzarelli, eds., *Struggle for Power in Education,* The Library of Education Series (New York: The Center for Applied Research in Education, 1966), chap. iv, pp. 49–66.

An Operational Definition

The author defines as "political" that *segment of social life involving the activities and relationships of individuals, groups, and associations resulting in, or intended to result in, decisions by any governmental policy-making body.* This definition leaves out much of the realm of social activity and power. It leaves out the consideration of those social activities and uses of social power aimed at influencing the behavior of governmental officers and offices conceived individually, such as a state commissioner or a local district superintendent. These offices and their incumbents are, indeed, political objects and figures. If our goal here were a complete definition (and more to the purpose, were this obtainable), we would then take these into consideration; but our purpose is to limit discussion. However significant the executive office and officers are in terms of their impact upon policy making and implementation, in general, in the United States at least, it is still the case that "policy" having the force of law rests upon the action of elected officials acting as corporate bodies. On the other hand, our definition will, if anything, open up more than we really know. Confining ourselves to policy-making bodies will suffice in this work.

In a recent text on governing American schools, Roald Campbell *et al.* stated: "Educational policy making at all governmental levels is immersed in politics and by definition educational policy making is political action." [7] Similarly, Roscoe Martin pointed out that, "Politics may be taken to concern (1) the process of governance within the schools, (2) the process by which the schools are controlled by and held responsible to people, or (3) the process of decision making as it relates to other governments. . . . Politics, therefore, may be said to be essentially a way of looking at the public school system and its management." [8] Ralph Kimbrough has taken the position that, "If the educational leader and his staff have any opinions about educational policies and take action accordingly, public education in that school district is involved in politics." [9] The author has spent most of the last two decades in public education, so that a school district not included by Kimbrough's definition may still come his way, but until then, based on Kimbrough's definition, the author's experience is that all school districts are steeped in politics, although not in the "party politics" customarily central to the mainstream of American democratic life.

---

[7] Roald Campbell, Luvern Cunningham, and Roderick McPhee, *The Organization and Control of American Schools* (Columbus, Ohio: Charles E. Merrill Books, Inc., 1965), p. 404.

[8] Roscoe C. Martin, *Government and the Suburban School,* The Economics and Politics of Public Education Series, Vol. II (Syracuse: Syracuse University Press, 1962), pp. 53, 57.

[9] Ralph B. Kimbrough, *Political Power and Educational Decision-Making* (Chicago: Rand McNally & Company, 1964), p. 275.

As Martin reported, many fail to see the vital and longstanding connection between politics and education.[10] This is even more apparent with those most closely involved in schooling; this should surprise no one because myopia in political matters for those closest to the realities has a certain protective virtue. One's sense of well being in the social universe is better maintained in ignorance, although one's safety and chances for success or survival in the political clash of interests are impaired. The politics of education are not only different from the general partisan pattern characteristic of the best political heritage in the United States, but tend instead toward the closed political heritage of the one-party Southeast with its internal factionalism.[11] This trend generally produces "invisible" politics which seldom benefit the society involved or, in the long run, those who "play the game." At the state level, Robert Marden, who reviewed the studies of 1964, noted "the total immersion of the state politics of the public schools within the total political processes of state government." [12] His position, while consistent with the history of the behavior displayed by leading schoolmen during the last generation, violates the verbal dicta of these leaders and their followers. "It is," said Marden, "when the leaders of the schools are most effectively *in* politics that they secure the largest share of resources for the schools." [13] Kimbrough, generally more concerned with the local level of educational government, has pointed out that "most basic policy proposals involve concepts of economics, social systems, finance, functions of government and business. . . . All major educational proposals tamper with those concepts giving rise to political activity." [14]

Charles Wilson, superintendent of schools in Grosse Pointe, Michigan, described himself (and presumably his colleagues in office) as "a rather skilled political technician in suburban educational affairs," and he felt it was beyond dispute that "the most important consideration in the superintendent's existence is winning the next tax referendum." [15] Keith Goldhammer found that school board membership was of great concern to the dominant power cliques.[16] "The school board was to a large extent self-perpetuating, but its capacity to perpetuate itself was contingent upon the ability of the power structure to sustain its supremacy in the face of challenge."

Neal Gross, in his study of 105 Massachusetts superintendents and 508

---

[10] Martin, pp. 53–54, 111–112.

[11] This subject is discussed in more detail later; *see* chap. 2.

[12] Robert H. Marden, "Essay Review: The Politics of Education," *Educational Administration Quarterly*, I (Spring, 1965), 54–55.

[13] *Ibid.*

[14] Kimbrough, p. 275.

[15] Charles H. Wilson, "Essay Review: The Politics of Education," *Educational Administration Quarterly*, I (*Spring*, 1965), 69–70.

[16] Keith Goldhammer, "Community Power Structure and School Board Membership," *The American School Board Journal*, CXXX (March, 1955), 23–25.

board members, listed individuals or groups exerting pressure on the schools in the following order, as reported by his respondents: (1) parents or Parent-Teacher Association, (2) individual school board members, (3) teachers, (4) taxpayer groups, (5) town finance committees or city councils, and (6) politicians.[17] Indeed, might not all superintendents wish to say, as Wilson said, "For every potential vote to destroy my administration, and there will be many, I know where and how to rally two, three, or four supportive votes"? [18] So indeed is it "naivete in its most banal and dangerous state," as Donald McCarty [19] said, when the notion of keeping education and politics apart is espoused by those who say it and who know no more than to mean it.

Still the bulk of the educationists cling to the words, if not the reality, the shadow, rather than the substance, and are almost incapable of thinking of politics *and* education except prescriptively as other than discrete and immaculately untouching worlds. The myth that education is not politics—or, stated presciptively, that either "education should not be involved in politics," or "politics should not be in education"—virtually ruled the minds of many professors of education and the public statements of educators even when the practicing schoolmen and professors, such as Paul Mort, were never quite so naive. Ignoring for the moment the prescriptive "ought" concerning the separation of politics and education, and paying attention to the realities of American life, education and politics are and have been inextricably related.

It is easy enough to document the continuing existence of politics in education and of educationists in politics at every level of government—local, state, and federal—using the definition offered above.[20] At the risk of becoming entangled in a co-professional quarrel, the author must note two beliefs which are central to his concern for the politics of education: (1) in American life at least, educational policies are inevitably the product of political activity, not excluding the most invidious definition of the term "politics," and (2) with all the weakness of the two-party system, seeking to continue political activities apart from the two-party system may become more dangerous for education than seeking activity closer to that system.

Historically, education and politics have been mixed, whether or not one takes the narrowest, most partisan, and negatively-laden connotations of the term "politics." The blatant use of partisan patronage, particularly in connection with building maintenance, is paralleled in education's history by the existence of salary kickbacks to board members for the

---

[17] Neal Gross, *Who Runs Our Schools?* (New York: John Wiley and Sons, Inc., 1958), pp. 19–22, 50.

[18] Wilson, p. 70.

[19] Donald J. McCarty, "How Community Power Structures Influence Administrative Tenure," *The American School Board Journal,* CXXXIX (May, 1964), pp. 11–13.

[20] Masters *et al.,* p. 1.

employment of teachers. Nor was political corruption confined to fiscally dependent school districts, political bosses, or partisan election systems. Reducing the concept of politics to this invidious meaning, however, raises some questions concerning the educationist's belief system which warrant attention.

If schoolmen mean "dirty" politics when they say that "politics" should be kept out of education, and therefore they are given their commitment to distinct elections both for taxation and for board members as vehicles for taxation, what implications exist for the educationist's belief in the American and British political party systems? The myth implies that the educational profession has come to reject the two-party system and the mainstream of American political life as too corrupt, and too unchangeably corrupt, to let education thrive in it. A corollary of the myth suggests that regularly elected representatives in American government cannot be trusted by educators; therefore, the welfare of children would require, instead, separate elections and agencies. The implications of this position and the inference to be drawn from such a belief system, supposedly held by those entrusted with the education of the American citizenry, make one want to laugh and to cry, so pathetically ridiculous is our condition. Where it counted, educators—already committed to public service and interested in the enculturation of American children—have rejected the chief political machinery for selecting those who govern!

Alternately, and these are not mutually exclusive interpretations, the myth may imply a tactic on the part of the profession for freeing itself from the customary framework of American politics so as to acquire a special advantage in the control and financing of education. If so, the "keep politics out of education" plea results in an attempt to reduce the effect of party politics on education and to enhance the effect of the profession's own political activities. This would be hardly surprising since one of the usual functions of a political myth is improving the position of its champions. But a special area, such as education and its representatives, can only have an advantage in political affairs when it is accorded particular recognition and has access to means for influencing political decisions not equally available to others. The existence of such advantages always leaves open the possibility that, if the representatives of the special area should lose this esteem, the mechanisms which they have developed and used may be captured by others. To illustrate, one consequence of special elections in school districts has been the small "voter turn out." So long as "friends" of education constitute the majority voting, this may easily result in the district's support for education's program. But it also means that a relatively small proportion of a given community's voters does, in fact, act for the school district. It means that a relatively small proportion of one's opponents can also capture the election, acting for the school district.

A political myth which is contrary to fact may serve a group best in a political struggle when: (1) the group which created it uses it, (2) others have come to believe it, and (3) the group does not itself believe in it as a description of reality. The public schoolmen in this country may soon find that their ranks are replete with people who believe in staying out of politics while others are no longer persuaded that politics should be kept out of education. Were this to become the case, educationists would soon discover that many of those political arrangements previously presumed advantageous for better schools have instead become liabilities.

A most fundamental assumption underlying this monograph is that politics have not been and will not be kept out of education. A related concern involves the shibboleth, "keep politics out of education." This entails two potential dangers: (1) an implicit rejection of the mainstream of the American political system itself, and (2) a loss of touch with reality—a self-seduction which is the most dangerous form of fascination. The prevailing pattern of educational politics, at state and local levels, pays tribute at once to this enticement of educationists by the echoes of their own voices and to that separateness of pedagogical politics from the two-party system. The last point may be illustrated, but not exhaustively, by an examination of education's special governmental and political arrangements.

Special Governmental Arrangements

If there is one statement which, by repetition, wearies anyone studying the legal arrangements for governing education it is: "Education is a state function locally administered." The statement refers to the "mix" of state sovereignty in education and the delegation, through constitutional or statutory provisions, of administration to local school districts. In constitutional law this meaning is clear. The state can wipe out local districts, although in some cases it might require revision of its constitution. In the cases of chartered cities having a so-called "contract" with the state, this ultimate form of state control becomes trickier, and perhaps impossible, so long as the supreme court sits. If one thinks of a range of local administrations extending from chartered units, on the one hand, to offices and officers locally situated in physical fact but legally hired, fired, paid, and directed from the state capitol, on the other hand, school districts fall between these two extremes; but the districts are nearer to local control than any other significant public service is today. A shield of local school-district voting behavior is typically interposed between the state policy-making machinery and the local schools.

The mix of state and local powers is a holdover from the eighteenth and nineteenth century in the United States. It has been superseded in many other areas of governmental affairs by more centralized state agencies, but school districts remain as the governmental operation most like a midwestern adaptation of the New England Town Meeting or like the operations of the *Music Man* set in *Peyton Place*.

School districts exist by virtue of state constitutional or statutory provisions for delegating and decentralizing control from the state's policymaking arenas, which chiefly involve the executive and legislative branches. With this decentralization and, to a varying extent, with a decentralization of taxing power for educational support, has gone the responsibility to finance local schools and, until recently at least, to undertake the lion's share of the costs. Futhermore, districts are governed in most instances by elected school boards; their number of members varies. As a result of the efficiency movement,[21] translated into government, schools, and churches, to make boards more efficient (as we now see), boards normally range from three to twelve members. School board members are usually elected for three or more years and, more significantly, as an arrangement to insure stability, their terms are usually staggered and overlapping. Thus, a board "take-over" would require control of at least two consecutive elections; however, this is not always necessary.[22] The staggered election pattern may act as a major stabilizing factor in educational government. That government may, in fact, appear to be static, but it would be inaccurate to attribute the stability of American education to these local school board arrangements alone. Such a system is likely, however, to place a high premium on doing what was done before, on inducting new board members into its operational mysteries by a seniority system of informal status, and, consequently, on maintaining the status quo.

Other statutory arrangements and some traditional appeals to emotion by members of the educational fraternity also have the effect of maintaining the status quo—in particular, the arrangements for protecting education's professionals from interference in doing their job, and the arrangements for "keeping politics out of education." These are not mutually exclusive categories. Indeed, the education professional can claim not only, "What's good for General Motors is good for the nation," but more happily, "What's good for teachers is good for our children." Specifically, the existence of such arrangements as superintendent contracts, teacher tenure, and the recent legal sanction for negotiations constitute examples of legal means for reducing the vulnerability of school people before the public. While this sort of protection ought to make innovation more possible, actual events suggest that a professional or craft group will neither innovate nor adapt new measures unless external pressure is applied to its organized members.

---

[21] This efficiency movement was subsequent to Louis Brandeis' use of the principles on scientific management by Frederick W. Taylor; Brandeis used this information to prevent the railroads from getting a rate increase between 1910 and 1914.

[22] *See* chap. v for exception.

Hence, arrangements to protect schoolmen and teachers tend to maintain the status quo and to provide a special brand of politics.

Special Political Arrangements

A number of typical arrangements for carrying on the political life of school districts now link "keeping politics out of education" with the welfare of children in the public's view. These arrangements include such features as holding separate school elections. Often this eliminates overt party politics in school affairs, although it has less effect upon the relationship of precinct and ward machines to such educational matters as expenditures for custodial operations than the overt activities would suggest. The replacement of the two-party pattern of nomination for office with the establishment of a single nominating committee or caucus consisting of disinterested (*sic*), civic-minded, distinguished community leaders, again, in no sense keeps politics out of education. It does tend to remove the politics of education from the general American pattern of the two-party system, and it produces a special brand of politics—the politics of education.

School systems with their legal structure of boards, administrators, and teaching staffs increasingly tend to be encased in a network of extra-governmental friends and allies. A civic cocoon of advisory groups, lay committees, parent-teacher organizations, grade mothers, Girl Scout Brownies, and athletic boosters surround, politically protect, and nurture the local educational leaders in school district matters. Whatever the original intent, the operating definition of keeping politics out of education has had significant consequences in addition to removing educational politics from the American two-party pattern. These are better understood if one recognizes the emotional content education carries in American communities.

"What they are doing to your children?" is one of the recent emotional appeals used in the endless public controversies over education.[23] Beyond reading, writing, and figuring, school controversies involve motherhood and little children, religious beliefs, churches, sacred rural values, the Star Spangled Banner, individualism and social concern as well as little red school houses and split-level dream houses surrounded by white picket fences. How, indeed, as Masters *et al.* pointed out, can anyone be politically against education? [24] Rooted, nurtured, and hedged about with sacred values, the politics of education continues largely apart from the two-party system. Without its elements of the sacred community, the elimination of the two-party conflict would tend to result in creating either a political area of endless factional struggles or one controlled overwhelmingly by a single

---

[23] Iannaccone in Lutz and Azzarelli.
[24] Masters *et al.*, p. 266.

faction with its network of groups. Given the sacred values involved in the case of education, the latter most often happens. This reduces public controversy over educational matters to what Arthur Vidich and Joseph Bensman described so well in Springdale as "The Etiquette of Gossip." [25] It is the politics of the polite priestcraft rather than of the marketplace which characterize the politics of education when schoolmen carry the day in public affairs. At both state and local governmental levels there are times when the politics of the marketplace, the competitive struggle of the hustings, and even, on occasion, the re-entry of the two-party system in the political struggle over education, do break through. Then the kaleidoscope of strong feelings, the rejection of euphemisms, and the clash of the established power structure against a challenging power structure is seen and heard. Then the great debate over curriculum, for example, is heard in public. So long as the politics of education takes its normal course, the open discussion of educational decisions is eliminated. Avoiding the two-party system in school districts has often carried with it the penalty created by the lack of a loyal opposition and, with this, the destruction of the system's capacity for self-criticism. The nature of the politics of education is characteristic of a relatively closed society.

At the state level, too, the mainstream of American politics, as typified in many states by the two-party system, has been largely avoided by the politics of education. Here, too, where the politics of education stand most completely apart from the mainstream of American politics, the tendency toward developing a closed system is found. Masters *et al.,* commenting on the state politics of education, concluded from their study of three midwestern states that there was no political coinage in education.[26] Subsequent developments in California showed that this statement was not always true. In general it is true, however, because the dominant pattern of state educational politics displays a relatively closed system of social power and politics. The dominant pattern of pedagogical politics at the state level also displays the tendencies toward: (1) the elimination of even a loyal opposition, (2) a reward pattern for maintaining the status quo, (3) the absence of adequate self-criticism, and (4) the establishment of an internal educational power elite. Nowhere at the state or local levels is this as obvious as in the case of the urban school districts, nowhere has it been as stultifying for schools as in the cities,[27] but the tendency to produce closed political systems appears wherever the politics of education are found, even inside education's own associational politics.[28]

---

[25] Arthur J. Vidich and Joseph Bensman, *Small Town in Mass Society* (Garden City, N.Y.: Doubleday and Company, Inc., 1960), pp. 43–48.

[26] Masters *et al.,* p. 275.

[27] *See* chap. 2.

[28] *See* chap. 2.

Systems: General and Political

Efforts by a number of scholars interested in theory—especially in theory for biological, psychological, and sociological phenomena, as well as for physical phenomena—have elaborated the general systems theory.[29] A system is defined as *a complex of elements in mutual dependence*. A system may be an element of a larger system. For instance, an animal, such as a buffalo, may itself be understood and studied as an organismic system and, at the same time, be viewed usefully as an interacting (mutually dependent with other buffalo) element of the larger group, which in turn is a system consisting of an animal herd. Thus, the buffalo in the illustration is at once (1) a *system* itself, and (2) an *element* or *subsystem* of a larger system (the herd). All systems known to man may be viewed as subsystems of a larger system and as composed of elements, which are subsystems. Any set of elements, whether tangible physical objects or fleeting conceptual configurations (including sets of social phenomena such as patterns of interaction in a political club) may be characterized by relationships of interdependence. This results in two additional generalizations: (1) When elements of a system change, their relationship to other elements must change, the nature of the set changes, and indeed, the other elements in the set also change. (2) A system will tend to retain the balance of relationships which characterize the dynamic interplay among its elements.

General systems theorists have found the distinction between open and closed systems useful. An open system is *open to its environment;* a closed system is not. In other words, exchanges take place between an open system and its environment consisting of inputs and outputs as viewed from the system's frame of reference. This is not the case with closed systems: an unchanging balance in the relationship obtained among its elements, called *equilibrium,* characterizes a closed system. Open systems tend toward a steady state instead of equilibrium. George Homans, in discussing "the small group," labeled this state *a moving equilibrium.*[30] The general systems approach offers a useful framework for thought and a set of concepts for understanding the politics of education. It has been applied to educational administration.[31]

---

[29] For examples *see* Ludwig von Bertalanffy, "An Outline of General Systems Theory" *British Journal for the Philosophy of Science,* I (August, 1950), 148; Gordon Hearn, *Theory Building in Social Work* (Toronto: University of Toronto Press, 1958); and James G. Miller, "Toward a General Theory for the Behavioral Sciences," *American Psychologist,* X (September, 1955), 513–531.

[30] George C. Homans, *The Human Group* (New York: Harcourt, Brace and Company, 1950).

[31] Daniel E. Griffiths, "The Nature and Meaning of Theory" in Daniel E. Griffiths ed., *Behavioral Science and Educational Administration,* Sixty-Third Yearbook, National Society for the Study of Education (Chicago: University of Chicago Press, 1964) pp. 95–118.

The following is Daniel Griffiths' summarization of the theory applied to educational administration:

> (1) Open systems exchange energy and information with their environments; i. e., they have inputs and outputs.
>
> (2) Open systems tend to maintain themselves in steady states. A steady state is characterized by a constant ratio being maintained among the components of the system. A burning candle is often used to illustrate one aspect of a steady state. Upon being lighted the flame is small, but it grows rapidly to its normal size. It maintains this size as long as the candle and its environment exist.
>
> (3) Open systems are self-regulating. In the preceding illustration, a sudden draft will cause the flame to flicker, but with the cessation of the draft, the flame regains its normal characteristics.
>
> (4) Open systems display equifinality; i. e., identical results can be obtained from different initial conditions.
>
> (5) Open systems maintain their steady states, in part, through the dynamic interplay of subsystems operating as functional processes. This means that the various parts of the system function without persistent conflicts that can neither be resolved nor regulated.
>
> (6) Open systems can maintain their steady states through feedback processes.
>
> (7) Open systems display progressive segregation. This occurs when an open system divides into a hierarchical order of subordinate systems which gain a certain independence of each other.[32]

One difficulty in finding an adequate conceptualization for describing the phenomena was noted by the ancient Greek theorists concerned with their government: overwhelmed by a changing world in the Near East, troubled over their sometime colonies coming of age, and faced with inter- and intra-city/state conflict, the Greeks saw their government seem to become immobilized into a condition of stasis or homeostasis. The notion of steady state, which is defined as maintaining a constant ratio among the components of a system, may be good enough for biological systems; it seems to lack something essential for social systems.

An additional property, noted by students of *social* systems, is that a system—composed of people ranging from the small group to the nation state with the bewildering range between—produces a "skin" or boundary line around itself. It may also work at maintaining that boundary. Perhaps it is more useful to view a *social system* as tending not only toward maintaining a steady state, but also toward equilibrium as it engages in boundary building and maintenance. Building walls to preserve a group's inner state is hardly a quaint old Chinese custom—it is closer to being the general rule of social groups when circumstances permit. Boundary maintenance produces a drift toward equilibrium. If an open system can keep its boundary intact, it often seems able to strengthen it. Strengthening a boundary for

---

[32] Griffiths, pp. 116–117.

a group is another way of saying the social system involved is decreasing its exchanges with its environment. It is drifting into a splendid isolation, perhaps a freedom from external constraints, according to the viewpoint of its members (people who are the elements or subsystem). Under a variety of beneficent environmental conditions, the cost of that drift may not be apparent for a long time. The nature of the drift may be internally, a tendency toward equilibrium, and externally, a reduction of exchanges with the environment. These are precisely the characteristics which distinguish open systems from closed systems.

The social systems characteristic of education—from the elementary school teacher within her classroom to supervisors in executive sessions with the school board—display a success at boundary maintenance that seems unbelievable, whether produced by happenstance or by the rich gift of true ability once reserved to Plato's philosopher kings. The author suggests that the key to this dubious success lies in the special arrangements of constitutional law and tradition which characterize the governing of education in this country. If the drift toward the characteristics of closed systems, tighter boundaries, reduced inputs and outputs, and homeostasis do characterize the politics of education, it is not necessary to accept the foregoing explanation to see that the politics of education may be regarded as closed system politics. Admittedly, the term "closed" is used loosely.

Dimensions: Governmental and Social

Apart from the precise scientific definition, a political system can never become closed to its social environment. A few island cultures in Melanesia, the Eskimos and, for a time, some governments of priests have come close to isolating one dimension from the other. The fact is that *society changes.* At some times it changes more than at others; in some places more than others. At mid-twentieth century, we are witnessing social change of a rapidity, magnitude, and completeness that has never been known before. Education and its governance can hardly be expected to remain untouched by this social revolution. Indeed, the resiliency of public schooling in the United States against change and education's capacity to maintain—virtually intact—the work-flow patterns of the early 1900s and the nineteenth-century forms of government that are being carried beyond the second half of the twentieth century is little short of unbelievable! Only an awareness of how little change has actually taken place with respect to the resource inputs of education, coupled with a grasp of how thoroughly the politics of education have been hedged about by special legal and extra-legal arrangements make these outmoded patterns understandable at all. But the society is changing, and the change in its public educational enterprise is beginning to accelerate. Thus, a dynamic relationship between the governing of education and the society is ripening between two dimensions—societal and governmental. We are particularly concerned with change in each dimension and in the relationship between them.

Government. The governmental dimension is characterized by the alternation of (1) *long periods of stability* with (2) *shorter periods of abrupt change*. This is the case whether one thinks of the governmental dimension in terms of its customary structure of organizations and the alignment of these, its predominate life style, or the characteristics of its governing elites. The pattern of change characteristic of the governmental dimension may be intermittent, displaying over time, as it were, stretches of homeostasis broken up by quick readjustments. Perhaps the pattern is most easily examined through the general constitutional arrangements which various states have for producing their legislatures. Resulting from an election reflecting the behavior and putatively the wishes of voters, a legislature is constituted, i. e., placed in office and organized internally for a period of two years. From one election to the next, stability rather than change characterizes this governmental body. This becomes even clearer in cases of governmental bodies, such as the United States Senate and certain school boards, where only a third of the membership turns over at each election.

The intermittent pattern of longer periods of stability and shorter periods of change is the basic rule.[33] While this example may be the most obvious, it is also one of the least significant instances of the intermittent change pattern operating in government. A realignment of political forces does not occur with each state legislative election. Except for technicalities, a reorganization of the internal power structure of a legislature, which might result from a change in the speakership, majority and minority leaders, and the key committee chairmenships, does not take place at the beginning of each legislative session. Still less does each school board election result in a realignment of forces with redirection of school board policy. But such realignments of forces, redistributions of political power, and redirections of policies do take place at both state and local governmental levels. When these occur, a sharp shift may take place in the government of education. The alternation of longer periods without such shifts and shorter periods displaying these changes make up the intermittent pattern of change in the governmental dimension.

Society. The societal dimension is, instead, characterized by *a relatively more constant rate of change*. While this rate appears to be moving faster during the present decade, it does not display the abrupt shifts and then

[33] The facts of elections in America and elsewhere illustrate, but do not alone account for, the intermittent phenomena here discussed. This pattern is deeply established in all social systems and is probably necessary, not only for man's psychological welfare, but for his task achievement as well.

stable periods seen in the governmental dimension. It moves more or less steadily, whether we use examples of social class mobility or geographic mobility. Similarly, economic phenomena, first reduced to numbers and then to line graph, display frequent hills and valleys as plateaus. Key differences in the several aspects of these two dimensions may appear too obvious to mention. The key to the governmental pattern lies in the artificial, consciously man-made arrangements for reflecting the society's needs, aspirations and wishes. So vast and complex are the population and interests falling within the purview of its government, that a huge universe of law and custom, as well as governmental bodies and extra-legal associations, have come into play, translating and transmuting the societal dimension's imperatives into governmental action.

These two dimensions are closely related to each other and they exist in a state of mutual dependence. For example, governmental decisions having the force of law hold a powerful effect over economic and social developments. The society's developments are repeatedly reflected in governmental action and are especially visible when an abrupt shift in the governmental dimension takes place. This is equally true in the governing and politics of education and in any other area or unit of American government. The special arrangements for governing education do make a difference, not to the general rule itself, but in the specific results when this rule is applied.

Relationships. Implications of the relationships between these two dimensions are probably numerous, but most of them do not concern us here. One major implication does. We begin by thinking of each of the societal and governmental dimensions as abstractions, identifying two vast and complex social systems in mutual dependence, even in the case of school districts. This suggests that their respective patterns of change, existing as mutually dependent, will predict one of two particular dynamic relationships between the two systems: (1) An abrupt shift in the governmental system, occurring when a well-organized revolutionary minority occupies the offices of government, may produce a large gap between the governmental system and its society. While hardly as dramatic as revolution, the sudden take-over of a school board by a well-organized and well-financed minority is not unknown in American communities, especially in suburban areas. A shift of the governmental system produced by such a minority will almost always result in a wide gap between the social and governmental systems. Unless another quick shift occurs in the governmental system reversing the take-over, convergence over time between the governmental and social systems will take place.

(2) More often, particularly regarding education in the United States, the converse will develop. Given the intermittent change pattern of governmental systems and the more constant or steadier changes of the

larger social system, divergence and a widening gap between the two is likely to take place. Then we will find political action by members of the society bringing the governmental systems into line with the social system.

The intermittent pattern of change in governmental affairs tends, thus, to be a consequence of the relatively sociostatic nature of governmental systems, reflecting their artificial arrangements, *and* the more constant rate of change existing in the larger society. The explication of the relationship between the two systems, particularly concerning changes in this relationship between them, rests upon the virtually inexorable bent toward repetitive behavior and constancy in governmental systems.

Governmental systems with their political subsystems which tend to be relatively closed have already been described as lacking, especially in respect to their capacity for self-criticism. The concept of self-criticism applied to governmental and political systems is semantically laden with euphemism. But the more open a governmental and political system is, the more efficiently it meshes with its societal environment, at least with its ease in receiving societal inputs. This is precisely the theoretical distinction between truly open and closed systems. One exchanges inputs and outputs with its environment; the other does not. Using the concepts of openness and closedness loosely, as we have, the difference between relatively open and closed political systems lies in their capacity to *accept* or *reject* societal inputs.

Special governmental arrangements, both state and local, have, with regard to educational policy making, the effect of developing among educationists and school districts an amazing capacity for rejecting changes in social inputs which would modify their habits and their internal status structure. The rejection of new inputs, people, ideas, activities, technologies, and so forth by those who have the most to lose if only in the short run, where acceptance would disturb the internal power structure—the rejection is hardly surprising. What is surprising is the capacity for this rejection displayed by public employees, particularly in American education! In this connection, the absence of the two-party system, characteristic of the American political mainstream, is noteworthy, not because the author finds the two-party system magical or an end in itself—for it is mundane and merely a means to an end—but because that end is the *creation and institutionalization of a loyal opposition within education's political pattern.* To remain within the Anglo-American democratic tradition and to develop and institutionalize a loyal opposition within a public service area, where education exists, seem difficult tasks without the two-party device!

Relatively closed political systems, as school districts are in the American political milieu, will continue operating under the general rule of convergence between their governmental and social subsystems. Open political systems, while displaying shorter periods of stability, would have smaller gaps between changes, and less abrupt governmental shifts. Therefore, something of the flavor of a revolution—without bloodshed but with many destroyed careers—is likely to characterize the shifts in the closed political systems of education; whereas, creative change and fresh patterns would have a greater possibility of emerging through more open systems.

Illustration for this chapter's theses will be easy, but documenting evidence at the state level is limited. Only exploratory research involving twelve states has been reported in recent literature. Data from available research will suffice to give a crude picture of pedagogical politics at the state level. Better evidence on local school districts is established with verified and exploratory studies. These studies lead the author to conclude that the most beneficent task needed for the professionals in education and the society is *the political institutionalization of a loyal opposition inside the politics of education.*

CHAPTER 2

Politics Preferred by Pedagogues

The preferred politics of pedagogics is the politics of the priest-craft protected by its putative mastery of the mysteries of educational expertise, supported by the public's emotional response to sacred values, and proceeding within the privileged sanctuary of its private preserves. This pattern is not confined to dealing with "lay" persons; behavior characterizing the politics of education appears throughout the internal power struggles of educational associations as well.

Consistency between internal and external power patterns would be expected of any profession's life style. The tendency to develop a closed system of professional-association power structures is not limited to the internal politics of educational associations nor to the external attempts to influence governmental arenas. It is central to and the essence of the politics of schoolmen. Internally, it is found in the profession's family-power struggles and externally, in the largest local school district to the smallest one. The country and the schoolmen pay a high price for trying to make a governmental system become self-criticizing without institutionalization of a loyal opposition.

The National Education Association [1]

The internal power struggles of educational associations are not political in terms of our definitions.[2] A brief examination of one of the most intense struggles will: (1) indicate the consistency of the basic patterns of closed system politics; (2) footnote the statement that the preferred politics of pedagogics tends to strengthen the boundaries of its social systems, resulting in a narrow base of support, and to perpetuate itself and its internal power elite despite the needs of society; (3) clarify the fate of the loyal opposition within the association, and (4) indicate the effect of these struggles in producing a growing teachers union, which has become a serious threat to the association's hierarchy within the profession.

The National Education Association has been praised by its friends and condemned by its foes. Its own writers classified it as the profession's builder, as education's champion, as the best source of educational informa-

[1] Ralph D. Schmid, "A Study of the Organizational Structure of the NEA, 1884–1921," (Unpublished doctoral dissertation, Washington University 1963).
[2] Chap. 1.

tion, and as the classroom teacher's protection against a hostile society. On the other hand, its fraternal rival, the American Federation of Teachers, has considered it weak and vacillating, made up of administrator-dominated, timorous school-marms of either sex.[3] NEA's foes accuse it of being unwilling to take a firm stand on controversial issues, unable to set educational standards, uninterested in quality except for verbal and slogan uses, and impotent insofar as improving the condition, the training, or the qualifications of its rank and file.[4] Each of these positions contains more of the truth than the representatives of the opposite camps will admit. This chapter will not draw a conclusion about either camp's appraisal. At a time when certain members left the NEA to give the AFT its first real lease on life, the events of NEA's internal power struggle revealed the closed-system nature of the association.

Between 1884 and 1907 the NEA was firmly controlled by a group of school superintendents and college presidents who became known editorially and conversationally as the "old guard" and which included W. T. Harris, United States commissioner of education; Nicholas Murray Butler, president, Columbia University; and F. Louis Solden, superintendent at St. Louis. They controlled it (1) through key positions in its administrative organization, and (2) by controlling the membership and offices of its two most influential subsidiary organizations—the Department of Superintendence and the National Council of Education. Two insurgent groups challenged their control.

The first group, consisting of superintendents, normal school administrators, and educational journalists headed by Carroll G. Pearse, superintendent at Milwaukee, and A. E. Winship of the *Journal of Education,* demanded that the NEA "old guard" open key offices to give them a voice in association affairs. The second group, leaders of the classroom teachers, demanded evidence of a greater concern for the classroom teacher and a more militant stand on their behalf. Margaret A. Haley, founder of the Chicago Teachers Federation, and Grace Strachan and Katherine Blake of the Interborough Association of Women Teachers of New York City led this group.

Occasionally during this twenty-three-year period, called the Butler era, insurgent groups combined forces successfully. Throughout the period they were able to make only slight gains. The "old guard" retained firm control of the board of trustees, the executive committee, the board of directors, and the corresponding offices of the Department of Superintendence and the National Council of Education. When the insurgent administrator and teacher groups fell out around 1907, the "old guard" was still dominant.

---

[3] Schmid, pp. 1–5.

[4] Myron Lieberman, *The Future of Public Education* (Chicago: University of Chicago Press, 1960), p. 182.

The "old guard" control reached its zenith between 1905 and 1907. This powerful inner circle met two or three times annually with the Department of Superintendence, the National Council, the board of trustees, and the executive committee. At these meetings and Butler's dinners, the policies of the association were set, the major decisions were made, and the offices and honors were parcelled out. The Department of Superintendence grew steadily in power, prestige, and importance. Decisions concerning the association were made at the mid-winter meeting of the superintendents and were implemented at the next summer's meeting of the NEA. By the turn of the century, the Department of Superintendence's meeting was commonly spoken of as the "most important educational gathering of the year," and was generally described as the "mid-winter meeting of the NEA."

From 1905 to 1907, the association's leaders manifested little interest in the material welfare of the nation's teachers. They listened to occasional addresses on the subject of salaries and passed a few resolutions dealing with salaries, pension, and tenure. The material welfare of teachers, according to the general attitude of the "old guard," was not a major concern of the association. The small group of leaders who controlled the association were firmly convinced that the organization served education best by devoting its attention to broad matters of policy, for example, through the Committee of Ten and studies of the economy of time in elementary schools. By and large, the classroom teachers were not active participants in NEA affairs. Only a few unimportant offices had gone to them and they were notably absent from the programs.

In 1909, the insurgent coalition worked together to elect the president of the association, and in 1910 they elected the first woman president, Ella Flag Young, despite the opposition of the "old guard." The insurgent coalition went on to capture the citadel agencies of the NEA dominated by administrators. Combining the voting strength of the two largest classroom teachers groups from New York and Chicago, the coalition was victorious. Once the insurgent administrators occupied the key offices, maneuvers by Carroll Pearse set the New York and Chicago teachers to squabbling among themselves and prevented a stable coalition. Together the teachers could have mustered enough votes to control any business meeting and to elect whatever officers they chose, except in Utah, for instance, or some other inaccessible place with large numbers of poorly paid teachers. But who would have thought of a national teachers meeting in Salt Lake City during the first half of this century?

By 1915, leaders of classroom teachers, especially in large cities, were turning to organizations made up *exclusively* of teachers. In spite of charges and edicts by school boards and legislators against such "unprofessional" action, city teacher organizations began to affiliate with labor unions. In 1916, the Chicago Teachers Federation affiliated with the American Federation of Labor, and that March, the New York teachers organized toward a similar affiliation. Within three years, the teachers union movement spread to thirty large city associations from New York to Los Angeles. The schism created between the nation's two largest teachers groups by Pearse in 1912 appeared to be closing in an organization outside the NEA. The AFT effort to give the classroom teacher a voice in the conduct of educational affairs was considered by the NEA a threat to the status quo in the association and a professional menace to local school board administrators. Inside the NEA, a reorganization plan, designed by Carroll Pearse in 1915, proposed: (1) to strengthen the victory of the Department of Superintendence over the National Council of the NEA and subsequently to defeat Pearse's sometime allies; (2) to put the control of the association permanently out of the hands of the active members; (3) to forestall the capture of the local associations by teacher unions, and (4) to put the NEA on a firmer financial foundation. The plan was supported by the former insurgent administrators and was bitterly opposed by Margaret Haley and the classroom teacher leaders when it was presented to association members in 1917. It robbed the rank and file members of the association of the small measure of control they still possessed.

The leaders of the classroom teachers were able to delay the reorganization for a few years, but in 1920 they were defeated by the new management and by Pearse's political sagacity. The association was reorganized under the control of a representative assembly, which was in turn firmly controlled by state and city superintendents of schools. A possible uprising of active members, a device by which the new management had first gained control, was now precluded.

The next year, the Department of Superintendence, which had long been dissatisfied with its relationship to the NEA, was granted autonomy to determine its qualifications for membership, to handle its own financing, and to set up its own headquarters with a permanent secretary. With these changes, the department was no longer subservient to the NEA; at the same time, its leaders remained in control of the affairs of the NEA.

In short, once the coalition of younger school administrators and big city teachers had won control of the NEA, its constitution was restructured. This reorganization—ironically called the "democratization of the NEA" by its historians—resulted in the following: (1) the citadel agency of the school administrator, now the American Association of School Administrators, was protected from NEA control; (2) the NEA management, on the other hand, was controlled by school administrators, and (3) the representative structure was more rurally dominated, at the expense of the city teachers. American public education has had a sacred rural tinge, whether viewed by leaders in administration, such as George Strayer and

Paul Mort, by intellectual rebels in foundation study areas, such as John Dewey, or by platform performers selling "progressive teaching," such as Professor Hill, of *The Music Man*. This disposition of *Gemeinschaft* in education continues into the last half of the twentieth century and heavily influences the professional, though not dominating him as fully at all levels as it did earlier in the century.

From 1884 to 1920, the sacred rural-community values dominated American education. Throughout the same period, the NEA had little to offer the classroom teacher. From the first, NEA management took the stand that a concern for the material problems of the teacher was not the purpose of the association. It seemed too crass. The type of problems faced by Charles W. Eliot of Harvard, Butler, Solden, Harris and the others who led the association, were not related to teacher salary or rights. They had to decide how to elect candidates from the growing public high schools for admission to their colleges or how to organize the relationship between the high school and the elementary school. These and other serious problems of national scope and importance were determined by the association. In effect, an extra-governmental association of interested parties took over where the united governmental structures, decentralized to an extreme degree in educational affairs, could not deal with the problems at a national level. The Carnegie Unit for measuring courses, the efficiency of time in the elementary school studies, the cardinal principles in curriculum, and the early junior high school, created to fill the gap between the six-year elementary school and the college-entrance high school, were all significant achievements for the NEA. The college president and large city superintendent elite, as well as the small midwestern superintendents, led the association to meet a real need in the country. These men overlooked teachers' real needs which were not immediately obvious. They did not live daily with such problems and considered salary discussions mundane. They saw the "big picture," and after all, the superintendents and presidents were *not* themselves grossly underpaid public servants.

During the entire period from 1907 to 1920, the power and prestige within the association gradually and steadily shifted from the National Council of Education, earlier perceived as the most august body of educational philosophers in the country, to the Department of Superintendence, the organization of the "realistic, practical, businesslike" superintendents of schools. In this process of change, *the NEA became a device for controlling the nation's classroom teachers*. Much of the leaders' energy after 1900, which might have been used to build a profession and a professional association, was expended for controlling the organization and its membership and in building the association *for its own sake*.

When J. W. Crabtree was named permanent secretary in 1918, the association's criterion of success became *the value of growth*. The new headquarters in Washington, D.C., and the growing permanent staff launched a drive for new members using the influence of the school administrators to coerce teachers to join. *Growth* became the major activity of the association.

In the early part of this century, the National Education Association was not "professional" in the sense that the American Medical Association or the American Bar Association are professional. *Peers* make up these organizations to *promote the cause of the profession* and protect the interests of all their members. Historical evidence suggests that NEA's critics were right when they said it was administrator dominated. It was almost inevitable that it viewed the world through administrative glasses. Surely, it was not likely to develop a vigorous program to improve the economic status of teachers. The group which eventually ruled the association, pulled by its immediate need to *run* schools, was unwilling to face the costs of serious professional training for teachers equal to that attained in law or medicine, and unwilling to fight for the kind of trained professionals who would, in turn, demand professional pay. Furthermore, the superintendents following Pearse's leadership were not educated men as Eliot, Butler, and Harris had been.

The critics do overstate their case and ignore what the NEA has done. It *has* taken a strong position on some key issues in American education, fighting these to the last ditch. For example, the NEA successfully instigated major curriculum changes in American schools during the Butler era. Reports of the Committee of Ten and the economy of time in the elementary school were especially responsible for these results. The Carnegie Unit, the present junior high school, and the kindergarten through sixth grade elementary school are in large part the product of those developments. These changes helped with the problems of college entrance and college articulation with the public schools, which were of major concern to Butler, Eliot and the men who held the association's power citadels at the turn of the century.

Dominated by the superintendents under Carroll Pearse, first the Department of Superintendence and later the AASA (American Association of School Administrators) led the association in the struggle for state aid. Early NEA research bulletins in the 1920s supplied superintendents with data to influence legislatures. The bulletins still do. With the help of key professors in educational administration, formulae for state aid to local districts were refined and put into law. These victories at the state level have their ironic side. Schoolmen interested in better financing for education fought the right fight but in the wrong arenas—state legislatures and local school district elections. They gained a larger percentage of state monies at the same time the states were getting a smaller percentage of taxable wealth. This situation paralleled Alice's predicament, as the White Queen's pawn, where it took all the running one could do just to stay in the same place. In the process, leaders of urban-classroom teachers were effectively shut out of the association's power structure which more and more resembled closed power systems. Urban teachers suffered under more than one relatively closed system.

The Urban School

The suburban development in the United States did not consistently produce quality schools until 1925. Indeed, through World War II, a teacher licensed in New York City could confidently apply for a teaching appointment in a Westchester or Long Island suburb, evidence that the suburbs not only needed teachers, but looked to New York City as equal to or above other sources in quality. The flow of experienced teachers from the large city to its suburbs has been characteristic of other metropolitan areas. The quality of teaching and the amount of education characteristic of teachers in the large American city was probably above the general pattern of the rest of the nation. Today the converse is true, with respect to the quality, if not the flow, of teachers. The usual explanations for this changed state of affairs, before it was called a flight from the cities, involved the identifying factors such as the automobile which made commuting easier, the love of trees and grass, and the desire to be closer to one's government and schools. The schools' reputation and quality may offer the single, most powerful explanation for the flight from the city. The evidence, both among parents still leaving the city and among those now returning to the city whose children have left home, suggests that, more than ever, the schools are the center of modern suburban development. If this is the case, then the changing nature of the urban pupil and parent population, usually offered apologetically by urban schoolmen for their difficulties, explains only part of the drop in the urban school's quality.

The quality of service rendered by public agencies cannot be explained by any one set of factors. The existence of expertise, its availability to the public agencies, the resources alloted by the public, the public's desire and demand for services, as well as the skill and morale of the public employees rendering such services, enter into the quality question without exhausting all possible factors. One set of factors certainly exists as a necessary element in providing the public with quality in any service area; it is even more necessary for continuing high quality. That element is found in the very nature of the political process available to citizens by which they can effectively wield power to influence policies and operations of a public service. This process deserves the most serious attention if quality is desired in public services and if that quality is defined in terms of the citizen's expressed wishes. A realm of philosophic issues and sociological problems of real importance involving the role of the professional in bureaucracies are raised by this problem and the political assumption stated above. But from the point of democratic doctrine, as applied in constitution and statute in the United States (whatever covert extra-governmental and extra-legal patterns have come to be), the role of the educationist "expert" is not one of dictating to the citizens. The weight of governmental power is not given to the specialist except through the citizen. Thus, if the schools were central to the earlier suburbanization trend, as they are to the present flight-from-the-city pattern, then it seems probable that it was easier for people to leave the city for the education of their children than to change the city's schools. If a city's schools were, indeed, subject to public control and changed only with extreme difficulty, if moving out were easier than changing the school system, the urban school would resemble a closed organization rather than an open one in its internal operations as well as its external relations.

Consistent with the thesis offered in Chapter 1, which specified governmental arrangements to protect the schools from corruption, by taking schools out of the mainstream of American political life a closed political system is also produced whose educational elite would have a heavy stake in maintaining the status quo. Clearly this has happened. The extent to which it characterizes the urban school, and consequently deflects efforts to solve the problems of urban education, cannot be known in detail without more research. The urban school at many levels, especially in its personnel operations, has become a closed system that is declining. This process will end in one of three ways: (1) A part of the society may decay until it has fallen to a basic point where the school district involved will be opened, perhaps violently, and its internal power structure and educational elite drastically modified; improvement in teaching quality will result. (2) The urban school's internal political elite and power structure may modify its own operation. This alternative seems highly improbable. (3) Public education may be abandoned as beyond adequate modification within the American governmental system. Public support of private educational establishments would be substituted. This would mean the American public, without abandoning education, would be abandoning its governmental pattern of education, for example, by continuing public support apart from public control. The closing system of American education would thus end where such systems do, if they are unchecked in their course toward closedness—deprived of all exchanges with its environment.[5]

The latter development seems less likely to the author than the first, the relatively violent upsetting of the school system within the context of its

[5] Daniel E. Griffiths et al., *Teacher Mobility in New York City* (New York: Center for School Services and Off-Campus Courses, School of Education, New York University, 1963).

social and political environment. The reformation from within seems even less likely, since urban school people feel their problems are easily solved by a new set of students and more dollars. When an unfamiliar problem is automotically viewed as "solved," given more resources, and a return to old problems, the schools are displaying Thorstein Veblen's "trained incapacity." The system under consideration is then almost certainly closed, lacking in capacity to view itself critically, and most in need of a loyal opposition but least willing to grant one a hearing.

The New York City schools present an excellent illustration of this last thesis. The largest public school system in the United States is not a typical system for reasons quite apart from its size. Nevertheless, it footnotes the point well. Pursuant to the shibboleth of keeping politics out of education and, precisely, to protect the school system's professional personnel from the evils of political patronage, the New York City school system's Board of Examiners was established in the late nineteenth century. This board, now consisting of eight examiners and the superintendent, is entrusted with the licensing of teachers and administrators in the city's schools. These include licenses for department heads, assistant principals, principals, supervisors, etc. It functions under an assumption that preventing patronage carries with it, almost mystically, a guarantee of merit or quality. Nothing could be farther from the truth!

Initially, New York City had quality teaching. Early in the twentieth century, salaries and other perquisites for teaching in New York City were among the best in the nation. The depression of the 1930s made teaching more economically attractive than it has been during the period since World War II. When teaching in New York City was attractive, the New York City schools began expanding their testing system for a variety of licenses in education, under the guardianship of its board of examiners. This system has become staggering. The system of licensing, based upon a formidable series of tests stretching over years for the higher licenses, created an examination marathon equalled only by the Mandarins of ancient China.

By the 1940s, the pedestrian nature of the examination pattern was decried as rewarding the plodder rather than the brilliant. Politically, no one could come to grips with the system. Members of the board of examiners were themselves a product of a similar system, removable only for cause and responsible by tradition to no one. Indeed, with only one exception during this century, no one—except New York City school people—has ascended the test ladder to the board of examiners, although examinations are technically open to outsiders. Consequently this special legal arrangement to keep politics out of the New York City schools has established a "test ladder" with the principalship as one of the higher rungs and the substitute teacher license as the lowest rung. In practice, this means that a fully licensed teacher anywhere else in the nation and New York State must begin with a substitute's license in New York City. Then he must not only teach but also prepare for a regular teacher's license to raise himself above the sixth-year salary step in New York City. Any student who would be fully licensed to teach in New York State when he left Cornell University, for example, would have to "surrender" the meaning of his state license, begin as a substitute teacher in New York City, and work his way through the regular teacher examinations. Similarly, if a teacher in Scarsdale, Winnetka, or Beverly Hills were inclined to accept the challenge of teaching in New York, he would have to begin with a substitute's license. Were such a teacher to exist, he ought to be re-examined for masochistic tendencies.

These special arrangements to protect professionals from politics have produced over 1,000 different licenses in education and corresponding sets of tests. The annual cost of testing applicants for teaching licenses is roughly *equal to the total budget* of the entire personnel operation of the City of New York! This ignores the personal cost to individuals as they prepare to take the examinations which are their only means of moving up in the system. This time and energy expended must be great indeed, because the examination system has produced its own special kind of "maze brightness."[6] "Cram schools," often taught by the New York City supervisors, cluster around the system. A few years ago, coaching tuition for the regular teacher's license was $300, and $500 was the reported rate for the principal's test. The city's book stores are well stocked with separate volumes on how to pass various examinations: that for the regular teacher, the department head, the assistant principal, and the principal, as well as others.

Expensive as the system is for the examinees and the school system, its effects are not beneficial to either. Faced with an increasing shortage of teachers, a simplified substitute teacher's examination was developed and is currently used. This examination insures little more than some basic literacy with any college degree as a minimum standard of admission to the classroom teacher's role. For example, by the 1950s, over twenty per cent of the classroom teachers were not licensed as regular teachers; they were licensed as substitutes. Early in the 1960s, thirty-three per cent of the teachers were licensed as substitutes, and now about forty per cent of the classroom teachers in the largest school district in America are licensed substitutes. New York City teachers do not qualify to teach in any other part of New York or other states.

Additional resources have been poured into an obsolete model, without changing it to fit the problems of a new day. The present system seemed efficient when New York City schools faced the problem of too many ap-

---

[6] Vance Packard, *The Pyramid Climbers* (Greenwich, Conn.: Fawcett Publications Inc. 1964), p. 13.

plicants for the positions open. It follows that the same system would be inefficient when schools faced the problem of too few applicants for the positions. The examination system drives people away. It did when there were too many applicants! The problem is subsequently more acute.

Many of the system's costs are less visible than those cited above, but no less serious. The examinations are locally developed and adjusted to New Yorkers; the higher one rises in the system, the greater is the premium placed upon experience in the city's schools. Local "maze brightness" is rewarded with a vengeance by the test pattern. This has the consequence of inbreeding to the point of incest. The necessary (but insufficient) conditions for getting into a principalship include: (1) being born in New York City; (2) going to the city's schools; (3) attending a New York City college; (4) starting a teaching career in New York City, and (5) staying there. How much more closed can a social or political system become?

School District Reorganization

Few political happenings illustrate historically the troublesome area of school district reorganization and unification so well as the process of self-criticism and internal readjustment does: how difficult it is to accomplish the process, if it can be accomplished at all; how rewarding it can be, if accomplished in time; how costly, if too-long delayed; and how seldom it happens, if ever. A local concern at first, the merging of local school districts in the interest of more efficient and quality education characteristically becomes a state political problem because local citizens, even when clearly acting against the best interest of their children's education, will fight all comers to retain their particular little red school house. Schoolmen, leading the fight for educational reform and governmental restructuring, have repeatedly called on the state legislature for action to half-bribe and half-compel the local school districts into mergers that would make the local operation financially viable, providing a range of educational resources impossible to former component units. The pious wish, written by H. Thomas James, in contrast to the actions of the legislature, makes this point. California schools districts

> . . . were designed to fit conditions existing at the time of their creation and they may need reorganization as new conditions arise. A board of education, therefore, has a responsibility to examine the structure of the district from time to time, and to observe whether the way the district is organized is the best way to provide educational services.[7]

[7] H. Thomas James, ed. *Boardsmanship: A Guide for the School Board Member*, The California School Board Association. (Stanford University Press, 1961), p. 37.

California was no different from the majority of the states that required "carrot-and-whip" legislation to produce changes by the state before significant local district reorganization and unification took place. The consistent need for state intervention in political affairs of the local district has usually been combined with grants-in-aid and negative sanctions to effect such mergers.

The position of the profession has been consistent with the action of the state. The American Association of School Administrators' Commission on School District Reorganization has declared that "the unified or twelve-grade school district which is adequate in size has proven to be the best system of school government devised by the American people." [8] Nevertheless, it has generally taken the power of the state, coupled with other financial incentives, to compel local school districts to reorganize. More to the point, the opposition to reorganization and unification has not come from the local public exclusively; instead, the professionals involved, the superintendents whose positions were at stake, have frequently led the political fight against unification. Their struggle against state house politicians has been unacceptable. The professional is leading a political struggle against the position of his professional association as well as the publicly-expressed wishes of the state. Such civic arrogance occurs when schoolmen are out of touch with political reality, fascinated by the echo of their own desires, and conducting private polls of their community's "wishes." Superintendents have awakened the day after a unification election to find themselves unemployed.

Irving Pearson noted some time ago, "Much of the opposition to reorganization is based upon considerations other than those most directly concerned with the child." [9] Nevertheless, the fact of state legislation, more or less mandatory in nature, has been largely responsible for the unification and reorganization accomplished to date. "Everybody is for reorganization for their neighbors." [10] Here is the nub of the problem! *Unification* is a governmental reorganization substituting a single government—the newly unified school district—for the multiple governments previously making up its districts. In turn, the politics of the newly united government will be different from that of its previous component units. Specifically, old component district power structures must merge, conflict, or collapse after multiple districts, boards and superintendencies reorganize into an effective

---

[8] American Association of School Administrators, *School District Organization, the Report of the AASA Commission on School District Reorganization,* (Washington, D.C. the Association, 1958), p. 92.

[9] Irving Pearson, "Factors Opposing Reorganization," *Phi Delta Kappan,* XXXII (March, 1951), 332.

[10] Eldon G. Schafer, "Unification: A Change of Power Structure Reflected in Board Composition and Superintendent Selection" (Unpublished doctoral dissertation, the Claremont Graduate School, Claremont, California, 1966), p. 93.

single district and set of offices. The existing power structure of a district often centers around the superintendent of schools, especially in small districts. He tends to lead not only the board and professional or allied groups encasing the schools, but also politically to gain active support for his program, which represents the best he can see for children and for himself, and often, what he cannot see. In the special world of the AASA during their February convention, Atlantic City hotel lobbies are filled with discussions by educational administrators who claim that resistance to reorganization is *always* local and the product of old-time residents, i.e. lay people who do not know better. But as Paul Mort has said, "In some districts progress will be made over dead bodies, literally." [11] He was talking about chief school administrators, not lay citizens.

Facing a specific district, local school reorganization becomes a political issue which invites sharp differences of opinion. Unification entails political realignment and the conflict implicit in this. The election of the first board after unification will be the most complete board election the new district will ever face, and the new board's first major act will be selecting a superintendent. Thus, the election of a newly unified district board and the selection of its superintendent both result from a highly political and relatively fluid set of events. If change and stress in social systems provide optimum conditions for understanding the basic processes which make them function, then studying school districts at the point of unification should explain the basic politics of education.

Eldon G. Schafer studied the effects of large, as opposed to small, changes in power structure upon the superintendency in districts immediately subsequent to unification.[12] Donald McCarty suggested that the length of the tenure of superintendents was likely to reflect how they fit the district's power structure.[13] Working with city managers—a group analagous to school superintendents—Gladys Kammerer and her co-workers found that city manager turnover was related to changes in political elites in their respective cities.[14] Finally, several of Schafer's colleagues were engaged in research on the superintendent resting, in part, upon an educational application of the Kammerer work. Together these led to Schafer's research. His *conceptual hypotheses* were based on an assumption that the superintendent's office is, in fact, political, and so tied to dominant community power structures that replacement of these with new structures resulting from

---

[11] Author's notes from a lecture course presented by Paul Mort, Teachers College, Columbia University, 1957.

[12] Schafer, pp. 260–406.

[13] Donald J. McCarty, "How Community Power Structures Influence Administrative Tenure," *The American School Board Journal,* CXXXIX (May, 1964), pp. 11–13. McCarty suggested more reliance on an external power structure than the author might.

[14] Gladys M. Kammerer, Charles D. Ferris, John M. DeGrove and Alfred B. Clubok, *City Managers in Politics* (Gainesville: University of Florida Press, 1962).

unification would, in turn, reject local superintendents as applicants for the newly unified superintendency. His *central hypothesis* was, as follows:

> The greater the power structure change reflected in composition of the first board, the greater the likelihood that the first superintendent of a unified district will be employed from outside the district.[15]

Here two strands of prior research were applied to the politics of education with an emphasis on change. The first, of course, was the Kammerer research cited above. The second extended Robert Freeborn's application of Richard O. Carlson's work on succession and the "career-bound" versus the "place-bound" superintendent.[16] Carlson found, under given conditions involving length of tenure of a superintendent, the immediately-previous position of that superintendent's successor could be predicted. An "outsider," a schoolman not in the district's employment at the time of his selection as superintendent, would more often be selected if the preceding superintendent had been in office for ten or more years. The converse was also true. Carlson believed the selection of an "outsider" indicated a desire for change by those on the board. Freeborn, who agreed with Carlson, also looked at different factors beyond the predecessor's length of tenure as a means of predicting the new superintendent's point of origin. Details of his work will be taken up later.[17] These two studies—dealing with (1) tenure and power structure changes in city managers and their councils, and (2) the inside or outside location of the new superintendents' prior position—were tied together by Schafer.

Arguments leading to his central hypothesis include:

> (1) The composition of a school board will reflect the power structure of a district.
> (2) A change in the power structure will affect the composition of a school board.
> (3) A change in the power structure tends to accompany unification of school districts.
> (4) Composition of the first board of a unified school district will reflect the extent of the change in power structure.
> (5) One measure of the extent of change in the power structure is the extent to which composition of the first board of a unified district mirrors the composite of outgoing component district boards.[18]

Moving from this, Schafer offered the hypothesis cited earlier. He elaborated the notion that a time lapse is required for any new person

---

[15] Robert M. Freeborn, "School Board Change and The Succession Pattern of Superintendents" (Unpublished doctoral dissertation, The Claremont Graduate School, 1966).

[16] Richard O. Carlson, *Executive Succession and Organizational Change* (Chicago, Illinois: Mid-west Administration Center, University of Chicago, 1962). *See* chap. 5.

[17] Schafer, p. 263

[18] Schafer, p. 262.

joining an organization to be seen, and, indeed, to become an insider. Following studies of an even larger number of districts, Schafer argued, "Time would be a factor in both a superintendent's forming strong political alliances and in terminating his services." [19] Thus, as an elaboration of his central hypothesis, he tested the following:

> When the first superintendent of a unified district is employed from inside the district (in conflict with the conceptual hypothesis,) it will be found that he was employed by his component district within two years of the first board election.[20]

In testing these hypotheses, Schafer used all the unifications from 1954 through 1965 within seven Southern California counties. Fifty-two unified districts were created during that time, but refinements of the research population led Schafer to eliminate seven districts, resulting in a sample of forty-five districts where tests of the hypotheses were conducted. Several different operational measures of "high" versus "low" change boards were used which provided separate but not unrelated tests of the hypotheses. For example, where many of the unifications followed a district's long history of operating in a closed manner and with basically common administration components already present, he found that his central hypothesis was supported at the .05 level of confidence. While this is higher than chance, it leaves much to be desired. The application of the two-year redefinition of outside men, i.e., adjustment for a time lag in becoming linked to the old power structure, changed the level of significance upward to .01. Using high-low change to mean years of board member experience, Schafer found significance levels of .01 for the unadjusted major hypothesis and .001 for those adjusted by taking the two-year exceptions into account. Identical significance levels resulted when high-low changes were measured in terms of number of defeats of component board members and when measured in terms of *percentage* of successful component board candidates. These are not the same, nor are they necessarily related mathematically, except in extreme instances. Considering the fact that a unified board of seven members frequently replaces previous boards with a total of from twenty to over thirty members, one could have a unified board whose entire membership had been on previous component boards although from thirteen to more than twenty-three prior members had been defeated. Finally, Schafer developed, *post factum,* a composite weighted board change factor by taking together his different measures and tests of the independent variable.

With whatever measure of changes in the newly unified board Schafer used, two things consistently resulted. (1) The similarity or difference of

---

[19] Schafer, p. 264.
[20] Schafer, pp. 266–267.

the first new district board to the component boards predicted whether one of the inside, component superintendents would be picked for the chief administrator's job or not. (2) In each instance, the level of significance of the findings increased by taking into account the two-year exception, which appeared to indicate how well established or how well tied in with the old crowd the superintendent of a component district was.

These findings are worth examining in reference to the theory offered in Chapter 1. "Given the intermittent change pattern of governmental systems and the more constant or steadier changes of the larger social system, divergence and the production of a widening gap between the two is likely to take place. Then political action by members of the society bringing the governmental systems into line with the social systems will be found." [21] With one fell swoop of an entire school board, the election provides an unusual test of the interaction between the societal and governmental dimensions in the politics of education. Usually, as the society changes, it must face mutual dependency with governmental structures; in general, it can capture only one or two seats to begin changing the school district's government. It can hardly rally the whole community at the point of restructuring the whole school district's government. The first election of a newly unified district's board constitutes the rare opportunity for reducing, perhaps briefly eliminating, the divergence between governmental and social structures, programs, and forces.

Where the high-change board appears, the magnitude of change in the new board's composition, as contrasted with old component district boards, indicates the rejection by the community of the old governmental pattern in its only directly elected representatives.[22] The meaning of such election results are clear. Why such a rejection did not take place earlier is less obvious. Why did component school boards represent the community so little that they were frequently rejected altogether at one election? Some degree of closedness of the school's political system—sufficient to end in an abrupt governmental restructuring, a redistribution of power, and a realignment of politics in education—must have been present. The key to that closed system condition may well be, as studies have shown, the individual who tends to lead the board and the pattern of government and operations which places him there. The chief school administrator's relationship to the closed political system of the component districts becomes more obvious when the subhypothesis designed to test for this phenomenon consistently pushes up the level of significance in every test instance.

In terms of research technicalities, an additional exploration undertaken by Schafer, although less significant on the surface, is probably of more

---

[21] It is not the case from Schafer's data that these incumbents do not choose to run, *see* Schafer, p. 289.

[22] Schafer, p. 338.

significance to the field's growing knowledge in the long run. By using certain items on a questionnaire, he uncovered the political climate prior to unification and the "leadership" positions taken by specific component boards regarding such unification. Since all districts in the study had unified after a vote by the electorate, the boards and superintendents who opposed unification present strong evidence of being out of touch with the political realities of their districts. Other measures of being in touch with the election district's political realities may be moot, but, after the ballots are counted on a specific, single issue such as unification, public representatives who oppose their constituency are simply out of jobs. By Schafer's own understatement, his questionnaire items indicated that "boards of education do not always reflect, by their policy decisions, the wishes of a majority of their constituents. Such a contention was supported . . . so far as official board action on unification proposals is concerned." [23] Thirteen of the unified districts included in the study had component boards publicly, overtly, and officially opposed to unification. Concerning the superintendent appointments that resulted from the unification in these cases, Schafer reported, "There were no successful candidates for first unified superintendencies from component districts, boards of which unsuccessfully opposed reorganization," [24] i.e., the voter's wishes were expressed at the polls.

The situation is not difficult to understand. The superintendents whose boards opposed unification almost certainly led their boards. These men and their boards were not persuaded by the profession's position regarding unification. In many cases they continued to oppose the change after the state legislature facilitated greater unification. They were out of step with their communities, whose wishes were expressed by the vote. The board members involved suffered defeat on the first unified board, and the superintendents, *without exception,* were passed over as superintendents of their respective unified districts. An outsider was appointed instead. Either they failed to see the handwriting on the wall, or, seeing it, they fought the future after the end was in sight. In the first instance one marvels at the schoolmen's loss of touch with political reality; in the second, at the component district's political structure and its capacity to fend off the inputs of its environment for so long. Each, in its own way argues the existence of the closed system in the politics of education as revealed by the particular politics of school district reorganization.

Whether the preferred politics of pedagogics is the internal power struggles of education associations, the boundary maintenance and urban parochial exclusiveness of the New York City school personnel system, or the struggle to protect the place and the semi-rural parochialism dis-

[23] Schafer, p. 332.
[24] Schafer, p. 334.

played in the politics of reorganization, it is closed system politics. The separation of education from the two-party system has not kept power struggles and political conflicts out of school matters. Instead it has only shaped the politics of education as the politics of interest groups which are most active at the state level.

CHAPTER 3

State Politics of Education

The constitutional position of public education is one reason for focusing attention on the state politics of education. "Education is a state function"—that statement serves as the most universal preliminary description of the public school system in America. This aphorism is amplified by: "administered locally." Each state, through its constitutional arrangements, judicial decisions, legislative and executive actions, as well as its local administrative agencies, provides the legal context in which school districts operate and exist. However dear to the local citizen's heart may be his community's school district, it is legally a creation of the state.

While the grant programs of the federal government now play a large part in public education, it will be a long time before their influence can outweigh state influence. Indeed, increasing federal support of education may strengthen rather than weaken the impact of state government upon schools for some years. For example, federal grants which extend the operations of state departments, as in California, are likely to *increase* the power of states over education. Similarly, if the recently established research and development centers continue to emphasize applied research and demonstration to the elimination of basic research, the new federal resources will, in effect, strengthen the old established patterns of control and operations. It is clear that such centers, dominated by local school administrators rather than students of education, will entrench the existing patterns more deeply. The recent educational compact among the states, advocated by James Conant and supported by the Carnegie Foundation, may be coopted by the educationist elites which are presently at the top of their respective state educational systems. It is improbable that the state will lose its dominant role in governing education through local districts in the near future. But the nature of the state politics of education may be affected soon by developments at the national level.

The influence of the state upon public schools and classrooms is not merely potential, in terms of the legal structure, nor even confined to the indirect influence of grants for consolidation. Public education at the local level continues to be increasingly dependent upon state monies for daily operation as more and more state revenue goes into education. The formulae for disbursing state funds for education establishes realistic boundaries of decision making by the local school boards and administrators. They are intended to do precisely this. Schoolmen have had a major influence in developing these legal controls of state aid. Despite the profession's traditional commitment to the local school district concept, this control has resulted from the political activities of schoolmen at the state governmental level. Beyond the immense and indirect state control, which the power of the purse places upon the local school district, lies the realm of direct legal mandate. The hazy folklore of schoolmen and their "lay committees" customarily underestimates and understates the role played by legislation in directly limiting and shaping educational activities. This is partly because a belief system treats what is valued as *reality;* the deep-seated value placed on localism in American life is not easily reconciled with the fact of state mandates in educational matters. In addition, state educational legislation varies; its particular elements are ignored in practice and overlooked by state officers. The realm of state educational mandate becomes amorphous, with some laws existing on the books, *per se,* and some laws governing very directly.

As suggested in Chapter 1, the political life of a society can display alternating periods of relative homeostasis and abrupt change. The United States has recently experienced rapid changes that have, in turn, affected the state and local levels of government. Education is caught up both directly and indirectly in these changes. The desegregation of education constitutes a major area of educational politics at all levels of American government. Implementing the federal decision in this area will be carried out by state or federal action. In either case, the consequences for the state politics of education will increase in spite of the present prominence of local, state, and federal conflicts in this area. Less direct, but perhaps more powerful in the state politics of education, will be the effects of integration on voting, regardless of temporary backlash.

One other event in the American political world cannot be ignored in this discussion. The Supreme Court decision on representation will lead to major changes in the power structures of a number of states and in turn produce major political realignment.[1] While the shadow of these coming events may lack a distinct outline to predict accurately, the political realignment at the state level is real and present. The state politics of education, the rules of the game, and the organizational structures and customary behavior patterns of participants will all be modified by political realignment in the states. Related changes will come suddenly and will be disconcerting for most educationists.

Legislation and Lobby

Within the universe of the state politics of education, particular attention will be given to the politics of the legislative sub-systems—educational

[1] In New York on occasion a stroke of the Commissioner's pen has sufficed.

legislation and the lobby. Recent research involving the state politics of education has been directed toward the study of educational legislation and attempts to influence it. The concern for educational change leads to studies of educational legislation over studies of state departments of education or state boards. Legislation first establishes the mandates followed by other partners of state government in education, and legislation soon changes them. The lobby has been called the fourth branch of government. The educational lobby will be one of the major concerns in this chapter and the next.

A typology by which a state's prevailing pattern of pedagogical politics may be classified rests upon the characteristic structural linkages between the state's legislature and the organized educational profession. Thus, the concepts which will be used to identify and classify the type of educational politics in particular states will be one of *organizational structure*. Correlates of political life styles and political elites will be noted with each type of organizational structure. In short, the politics of the pedagogical interest groups which are linked to the legislature are central to this chapter. Their leadership groups and the customary patterns of political activity, especially at such linkage points, will also be studied. Although the educational lobby may have sporadic success in a given state, it must match its organizational structure and political life style to the internal structure and decision-making pattern of the legislature to be continually successful.

In other words, this chapter is concerned with the organized profession as it actually goes about influencing legislation. The nature of the organizational structures which exist as links to the legislature influence the legislative process in regard to educational matters. To summarize, the focus here is on (1) the nature of the organizational link which ties the organized profession, in its political activities, to the legislature of a particular state, and (2) the educationist elite or the political life style of the profession's representatives at such linkage points. Priority which this book gives to the nature of the social organization, linking the profession's lobby and the legislature, does not assume that organizational structure is independent of the behavioral patterns of those who are its members. Mutual dependence—an interdependent interaction of the variables, of organizational structure, of characteristic behavior and leadership type—is assumed instead. However, it is easier to isolate and examine an organizational structure, such as cabinet, a state board, a committee, or a set of offices, than a pattern of behavior or a leadership group.

The author is aware that governmental and organizational units, such as those reported by Arthur Vidich and Joseph Bensman in Springdale,[2] do not always lie at the center of community decision making. The student

---

[2] Arthur J. Vidich and Joseph Bensman, *Small Town in Mass Society* (Garden City, N.Y.: Doubleday & Company, Inc., 1960).

seeking to understand the decision making process must look into informal groups and leadership cliques. Nevertheless, one cannot *begin* with the assumption that governmental units do not function at the center of decision making, and continue with the assumption that state teachers' associations, established largely to influence legislation, do not indeed so function but are, in turn, controlled by some invisible government. The beginning point, in establishing a typology of the politics of education at the state level, is to identify and classify the nature of the organizational structure, linking the professional organizations to the state legislature in order to influence legislation. Next, the political life style and leadership type found at such linkage points will be examined and treated as correlates of the nature of the organizational structure.

As suggested in the foregoing paragraphs, the lobby, while characteristically providing the initiative in originating bills and moving them through the legislative process, still depends on the legislature's structure and processes of decision making. Thus, the nature of education's associational system for influencing legislation will have to fit into the legislature's pattern to be effective, especially at the point of linkage to the legislative process. A legislature's structure for accomplishing its task is not likely to depend upon the social structure displayed by the lobby. Lobbies need legislatures far more than legislatures need lobbies!

If the relationship of legislature to the lobby is akin to the relationship of independent to dependent variables, then changes in the former will produce changes in the latter. To illustrate, assume that a legislature has the majority of education bills originating in the lower house where bills involving expenditure originate. Will the existence of a powerful, well-organized lobby in the upper house make much difference to the initiation of favorable bills in the lower house? Such a condition probably would give the profession's lobby the veto power over whatever educational legislation it disapproved, but no more. It would have to change its linkage structure to the legislature and tie into the lower house. The generalizations offered above with respect to change may also be illustrated by the following example: Assume that the normal pattern for originating and making decisions on educational matters followed the "civics course" outline; suppose that the lower house committee on education were effectively deprived of the power to originate or shelve bills as the result of a reorganization in the legislature's lower house, consolidating these decisions in the speaker's hands; then, to be as effective afterward as before, the educational lobby would have to influence the speaker's office as it once influenced the committee, hence changing the nature of its organizational linkage structure. Even a lobby with a perfect record would have to modify its organizational structure to influence legislation subsequent to legislative reorganizations when these occur. Political realignments and redistributions of power among the chief actors of the educational legislative drama, e.g., the executive, majority and minority leaders, education and finance committee chairmen, will have a similar effect.

Recent developments in the scholarship of politics and education offer greater opportunity for understanding the state politics of education than heretofore. Specifically, research supported by the Carnegie Corporation in the state politics of education has resulted in published descriptions of political processes clustered around educational law-making in eleven states, including *Schoolmen and Politics* by Stephen Bailey *et al.*[3] of the Maxwell school, and *State Politics and the Public Schools* by Nicholas Masters *et al.*[4] at Washington University. *Political Power of Education in New York State* by Michael Usdan[5] offers a study in the Empire State. These studies, constituting an important volume of theoretical information, describe the typical arrangements and customary patterns of influence used by schoolmen and their allies to influence the course of educational legislation in eight northeastern and three midwestern states. As Masters *et al.* stated, their work "yields no scientifically predictive generalizations."[6] This may have been inevitable during the early descriptive stage when the state politics of education was first explored. It may be the inevitable result of any study which is undertaken atheoretically. Concepts and theory may now be applied to the data which these writers have produced to promote a greater understanding of the state politics of education. At last, tighter theory and prediction with testable hypotheses and verificational research are feasible.

The area of state educational politics, which is central to government policy making in education by virtue of American constitutional arrangements, will soon witness significant change. At the same time, recent research developments permit us to clarify the concepts of politics of pedagogues which are useful and intrinsically rewarding for the following purposes:

(1) Our first purpose is to exploit the patterns of political activities surrounding education in the works of Bailey, Masters, and Usdan, particularly the political activities of schoolmen, professional educational groups, and school board associations as they influence the decision making of legislatures in educational legislation. We will be more concerned with public education than with higher education because the available studies are largely limited to the political activities of groups concerned with the

---

3 Stephen K. Bailey, *et al.*, *Schoolmen and Politics* (Syracuse, N.Y.: Syracuse University Press, 1962).

4 Nicholas A. Masters *et al.*, *State Politics and the Public Schools* (New York: Alfred A. Knopf, 1964).

5 Michael Usdan, *The Political Power of Education in New York State* (New York: Institute of Administrative Research, Teachers College, Columbia University, 1963).

6 Masters, pp. 9–10.

K-through-twelve "common school." Furthermore, this is the present area of action.

(2) Our next purpose is to generalize from the patterns of political activities of pedagogues, following Robert Merton's methods [7] with our own "theories of the middle range." These generalizations will rise from a comparative cross-section of eleven states with a relatively static viewpoint. A typology identifying four types of states will help us examine the process of political activity which educationists use to influence legislative decision making—an empirical typology to classify and discuss the eleven states.

(3) Finally, a longitudinal look at some of these states will introduce the element of history to develop a more dynamic frame of reference than our static viewpoint allows. Generalizations from this will lead to a developmental construct concerning the morphology of state systems of pedagogical political activities regarding educational legislative decision making. Descriptions showing where we are and where we have been and a developmental construct showing where we are going *do not by their very nature provide sufficient explanatory power to control the future*. They may be a useful half-way house on the road to explanation as temporary guidelines only.

Typology: Four Linkage Structures

The literature on the politics of education at any level of government is extremely limited. H. Thomas James [8] indicated the great need for research in the area of state educational politics. Ralph Kimbrough [9] stressed the critical role played by informal groups and informal interaction in influencing community decision makers who operate within the associational—institutional structure of offices. He suggested that the relationship of state to local politics of education depends equally upon the informal network and the formal structure of offices. Kimbrough realistically corrected the stereotype of the "civics book" picture of government. He checked the bias of educationists trained in prescriptive programs of the former era in school administration which was ruled by the hortatory eloquence of charismatic professors whose realism influenced their state and national roles in the associations but generally not their teaching. Kimbrough did not, however, provide a base for distinguishing informal power networks nor for explaining them so that changes could be predicted in them.

---

[7] These were described as "empirical generalizations"; *see* Robert K. Merton, *Social Theory and Social Structure* (rev. and enlarged ed.; Glencoe, Ill.: The Free Press, 1957), pp. 95–96.

[8] H. Thomas James, "Institutional Character of Education: Government and Politics" Review of Educational Research, Vol. XXXIV, No. 4 (October, 1964) p. 410.

[9] Ralph B. Kimbrough, *Political Power and Educational Decision-Making* (Chicago: Rand McNally & Company, 1964).

Structure of Key Link / Correlates	TYPE I DISPARATE (Locally-based)	TYPE II MONOLITHIC (State-wide)	TYPE IV SYNDICAL (State-wide)	TYPE III FRAGMENTED (State-wide)	
ELITE TYPE	Squirarchy	Oligarchy	Synarchy	Polyarchy	Section A
POLITICAL LIFE STYLE	Entrepreneurial	Cooptational	Coalitional	Competitive	Section A
GEMEINSCHAFT-GESELLSCHAFT CONTINUUM	Gemeinschaft Very high	Gemeinschaft High	Gemeinschaft-Gesellschaft Blended	Gesellschaft	
INFORMATION: Quantity	Small	Large	Large	Very large	Section B
Nature	Unscientific	Precise and Predictable	Precise and Predictable	Precise, but not Predictable	Section B
Control	Personalistic	Monopolistic	Monopolistic	Competitive	Section B

Figure 1. A Composite Chart of characteristic types of Organizational Structures which attempt to influence Legislation correlated to the Educational Association networks and the Legislature. In Section A, key linkage structures are correlated to Political Life Styles and Elites ranked on the Gemeinschaft-Gesellschaft continuum. In Section B, Linkage structures are correlated to the Quantity, Nature, and Control of Information, and ranked on the Gemeinschaft-Gesellschaft continuum.

The most comprehensive and stimulating research for understanding state politics and education were explored by the teams at Syracuse University and at Washington University supported by the Carnegie Corporation.[10] With the work of Michael Usdan,[11] these reports provide the only extensive research on state educational politics in recent years. Usdan was more detailed and more penetrating about the educational politics of New York State than the Bailey team, but the latter also studied the politics of education in New England and New Jersey. Illinois, Michigan, and Missouri were studied by the Masters team from Washington University.

Each of these studies followed a reporting pattern characteristic of political science, i. e. without explicit conceptual framework at the start. Unfortunately, this limits the communication of their work, particularly for applying generalizations elsewhere.

Several virtues are apparent in using the work of others, whether one uses a conceptual framework or a framework emerging from the analysis of their work: (1) the sense of discovery, which *post factum* analysis offers whenever it is undertaken, becomes a chase that can be carried on in one's own arm chair without tedious data collecting; (2) although pieces are frequently missing, "obvious" questions unanswered, and data too slim, such reports do allow one to escape the trees and see the forest more clearly than one may from the midst of political action or data collection; and (3) the task is important! Keith Goldhammer [12] pointed out that these studies will become more valuable contributions as soon as the concepts for dealing with them are explained and the relationships classified, i. e. after theory is developed. Theory building in this crude way is still the product of *post factum* analyses and far from trustworthy. It provides a basis for testing, but such theory must obviously be abandoned as soon as verificational studies supply stronger, more predictable data.

In each state the nature of the organizational link between the legislative process and the associational system of schoolmen is capable of description and classification. Because the published reports concentrated more on the action of the organized profession to influence the educational policy developed in the legislature than on the legislature itself, the classification of states here will employ the political behavior patterns of schoolmen pursuing their legislative goals as correlates of the organizational structural categories for linkage points discussed above. Leadership type (or elite) for each structural category, with its related life style, is an extrapolation from the concept of political life style as related to each type. The published data are

[10] Bailey *et al.* and Masters *et al.*

[11] Usdan.

[12] Keith Goldhammer, "Essay Review," *Educational Administration Quarterly*, Vol. I, No. 2 (Spring, 1965), pp. 68–69.

relatively slim and the author has drawn on his experiences in administrative theory as a guide.

Four types of organizational patterns emerge from the descriptions available. These are qualified within the limits of this chapter; obviously more types might result if a deductive pattern or reductionism were used to extend the typology. Furthermore, studies of additional states may result in descriptions with far different linkage patterns between the legislature and the association network of schoolmen. *A system which builds toward theory from an empirical base is not likely to be exhaustive.* On the other hand, the possibility remains that, as a middle-range theory, the typology here does not attempt to deal with the full range of state politics. It even narrows its focus of educational politics to *legislative* educational politics. More cogent yet, the possibility of eleven states showing the total significant variation of fifty grows greater as one takes into account the interstate network of schoolmen. One or two aspects of this phenomenon will be enough to illustrate the point.[13]

In 1923, the research division of the NEA produced its first publication—information comparing expenditures for education among the states. These comparative data provided an obvious basis for schoolmen from low-expenditure states to influence their legislatures toward matching the wealthier states. In fact, this had been the intention of the publication and remains the function of the NEA research bureau.[14] Its impact brought the actual expenditure levels of the states closer together, and at the same time provided a network for the legislative–association relationships from state to state.

The role of the "scribbler," noted by Bailey *et al.*,[15] is also important in standardizing what could have been dissimilar systems of operations and patterns of support from state to state. This role is so far-reaching as it travels the association networks that the California educational finance legislation was influenced by two generations of "scribblers" from the same New York City "shop"[16] in the 1930s and the 1940s. The drift has not always been from East to West. In the early 1950s "scribblers" from California, Florida, and Tennessee provided the expertise, professional prestige, and apparent non-involvement needed to include the junior college in Missouri's master plan for education.[17] "Non-involvement" by out-of-

---

[13] *See* chap. 2.

[14] J. W. Crabtree, "Forward," *Research Bulletin of The National Education Association,* Vol. I, No. 1 (January, 1923), p. 3.

[15] Bailey et al., pp. 23–26.

[16] George Strayer in the 1930s and Paul Mort in the 1940s; the "shop" was Teachers College, Columbia University.

[17] Laurence Iannaccone, "Future of State Politics of Education," Frank W. Lutz and Joseph J. Azzarelli, eds., *Struggle for Power in Education* (New York: The Center for Applied Research in Education, Inc., 1966), p. 54.

state consultants is the educationist internal half to the "non-partisan" external half in the politics of education. It follows that imported "scribblers," who were conversant leaders, comfortable with the expansion of junior colleges in California and Florida, could easily influence other states to adapt a similar pattern, as Missouri did in the 1960s.

The technique of using an extra-governmental association network of co-professionals for solving national problems in education is not dissimilar to the Compact of the States [18] as a way around constitutional barriers to a federal school system. Indeed, faced with problems of national importance and given a decentralized government structure, it seems inevitable that national extra-governmental patterns for standardizing education would develop by 1900. To a large extent, such a development reached full flower in the 1940s. The 1923 bulletin published by the NEA research division was a logical middle step as extra-governmental centralization of public education developed. The process was influenced and accelerated by Charles W. Eliot of Harvard and Nicholas Murray Butler of Columbia as their colleges wrestled with the problem of admitting students from public high schools shortly after the Kalamazoo decision.[19] Working through the august National Council of Education, Eliot, Murray and their distinguished allies dominated the NEA, which produced a multitude of studies during their leadership, e.g., the study that resulted in the Carnegie unit for counting credit hours in the high schools. The committees concerned with economy of time in the elementary schools led to revisions of the elementary curriculum, developed the K-through-six plan, and introduced the junior high school. The genesis of these reforms is evident in the problems posed by the universal high school and its graduates that Eliot, Butler, and others grappled with. The work of these NEA committees, initiated by academicians, was completed by the "practical" superintendents and normal school administrators, especially from the midwest.[20]

Evidence indicates that the education association network of power and influence used "scribblers" to produce studies, reports, and recommendations between 1890 and 1915 to solve educational problems common to the nation. A single, governmental organization did not exist to solve such problems, and the extra-governmental operation of the extra-legal associations of the educational professionals had to be employed. The similarity displayed by fifty legally-discrete and disparate state systems of education is one result of this *modus vivendi*. Each system looks much more like any one of the others than like anything else known to man. Summarily, it

[18] James B. Conant, Shaping Educational Policy (New York: McGraw-Hill Book Company, Inc., 1964).

[19] Stuart v. School Dist. No. 1 of Kalamazoo—30 Mich. 69 (1874).

[20] H. Warren Button, "Committee of Fifteen" (Mimeo paper, Washington University, 1961) discusses the costly implications of this institutionalized anti-intellectualism in American Education.

seems quite possible that the four types of linkage structure, found in the eleven states studied, may be all that do exist. Until more states are studied and described, the four types will be used.

The typology used turns upon the nature of the organizational structure, which characteristically links the network of educationist groups to the legislature. One may visualize a state legislature and the lobby—i.e., any set of organizations attempting to influence the legislative process—as a single, complex social system; so conceived, the legislature and the lobby are sub-systems of a larger system clustered around the process of legislation. The specific organizational units (offices, committees, and groups), which work as *key links* between the specific lobbies (and their far-flung tracery of social groups), play a central role in translating influence into the legislative process. Such a social unit, where interaction, takes place linking sub-structures that comprise a larger social structure, may be called a point of tangency:

> The linkages at these points of tangency occur in the form of dyads or face-to-face groups comprised of persons who hold common membership in two or more groups (within the social system involved in legislation, thus linking these groups to the legislature) by means of a network of interaction.[21]

To classify states in the typology, the key unit of social structure will be the usual point or points of tangency which link the association network of educationists and their allies to the state legislature. The interaction customarily taking place among those who occupy positions in this key-linkage point is used to identify the type of social structure attempting to influence educational legislation. Basically four patterns may be found in reports on the following states: Connecticut, Illinois, Maine, Massachusetts, Michigan, Missouri, New Hampshire, New Jersey, New York, Rhode Island, and Vermont.

I. The first type of linkage structure exists in Vermont, New Hampshire, and Massachusetts, although Massachusetts seems to fit the second type, too. Localism characterizes this structure and the customary interaction at the usual points of tangency linking educationists and the legislature. That is, the participants to the interaction, both legislators and schoolmen (but in particular the schoolmen), represent their school district first of all.

---

[21] Frank W. Lutz and Laurence Iannaccone, "Power Relationships and School Boards," *Journal of Education*, Karaidudi, Southern India, IX (October, 1965), 1–9. This concept is adapted from the Solon T. Kimball and Marion Pearsell, *The Talladega Story* (University: University of Alabama Press, 1954), p. 259; *see also* Frank W. Lutz, "Social Systems and School Districts," (Unpublished doctoral dissertation, Washington University, St. Louis, Missouri, 1962), p. 6; Laurence Iannaccone, "An Approach to the Informal Organization of the School," in Daniel E. Griffiths, ed., *Behavioral Science and Educational Administration*, Sixty-Third Yearbook, National Society for the Study of Education (Chicago: University of Chicago Press, 1964), pp. 234–238.

Localism implies the existence of geographic bases and districts as essential sub-units in the associational system of schoolmen influencing legislation. Therefore, a chief distinction between sub-units, the separation or boundary lines between sub-units of a structure, would be geographic. This type is locally based. Localism, denoting geographic distinctions and bases, also connotes an attitude of provincialism, jealousy, and fierce defense of one's home district against outsiders, especially against central government. Geographic separation among neighborhoods—the grassroots of the system of educational influence described in this type—is further reflected in the fierce independence of its units. Such a social system unites effectively to gain its ends with great difficulty when faced with extreme conditions. Even then it is likely to guard its independence jealously and to fall apart immediately after each victory. ***Locally-based disparate*** denotes this type of structural interaction linking the legislature and the association network.

II. The second type of organizational structure linking the legislature and profession is characterized by a state-wide pattern of interaction. Examples are: New York State, an outstanding case of this type; New Jersey, following the influence of New York State "scribblers"; and probably Rhode Island. Schoolmen customarily speak to the legislature on behalf of education. The chief distinction of the associational boundaries are interest lines rather than geography. The major components of the associational system linked to the legislature usually include the state school boards association, the NEA state affiliate, one or more state associations of school administrators, and some volunteer citizen groups such as the state PTA. Therefore, a chief distinction between the sub-units, the lines of demarcation among the component sub-systems, linked by points of tangency to the legislature, display a state-wide interest character. While representing different interest groups who could display a great deal of conflict and hostility, this type is also characterized by a high degree of consensus—a consensus mutually dependent with an organizational unit that represents the various state-wide interest groups of schoolmen and their allies. The result is a *pyramid* of associations interested in education and educational legislation—a pyramid whose apex appears where the associational system of schoolmen and their friends are customarily linked to the legislature. The *chief point of tangecy* between legislature and educational interest groups is the key point of tangency between the association and interest groups involved with schools. The social structure emerging from these generalizations is the feared, condemned, and over-estimated power pyramid such as the one found by Floyd Hunter.[22] It is a ***state-wide monolithic*** structure.

III. The third type of linkage is found in Michigan. Unique among the

[22] Floyd Hunter, *Community Power Structure* (Chapel Hill: University of North Carolina Press, 1953).

eleven states, Michigan contributes an empirically logical category. If a pattern of state-wide educational interest groups and associations, united into a monolithic structure, does exist (as in Type 2), then logically a pattern of state-wide educational interest groups and associations not so united may also exist. In Michigan the logical possibility finds its phenomenological reflection. Here state-wide associations of school board members, teachers of the AFT and NEA state affiliate, school administrators, and parent groups come to the legislature disunited, often in conflict rather than consensus, injecting separate, competitive proposals into the legislative process. ***State-wide fragmented*** describes this organizational structure and its characteristic interaction pattern with the legislature.

IV. Illinois provides the only instance of the fourth type of linkage structure. The organizational pattern linked to the legislature is state-wide, but the link is a formal governmental unit: the Illinois School Problems Commission. The SPC is a creation of the legislature. It functions like the better-known legislative councils.[23] Because Illinois adopted the legislative council idea in 1937, it is logical that the same idea was extended to educational matters. The purpose of the Illinois law creating its earlier legislative council is stated in its preamble:

> Such legislative planning and formulation as actually obtains would, by being recognized and made properly antecdent to regular sessions, conserve legislative time, save unnecessary expense, improve ensuing debate, and restore legislature activity to the high place in government and public which it merits.[24]

Twenty years later Illinois legislated the existence of the School Problems Commission. Masters *et al.* said that the legislature brought the commission into existence because it was "anxious to find solutions for the many problems in education it faced and to avoid the constant harassment that would result from failure." [25] Membership of the Illinois School Problems Commission illustrates its essential character, as the Washington University team stated:

> The salient feature of the composition and organization of the SPC is that it includes most of the major interests that have a direct and tangible stake in the outcome of the public school decisions. It is structured to provide these interests with a formal and official voice in its deliberations.[26]

Of the seventeen members, each serving two-year terms on the commission as the law provided, ten are legislators, five are appointed by the governor, and two (the state director of finance and the state superintendent of public

---

[23] Frederic H. Guild, "Our State Legislators," *The Annals of the American Academy of Political and Social Science,* CVC (1938), 144–150.

[24] Quoted in Guild, p. 145.

[25] Masters *et al.*, p. 112.

[26] *Ibid.*, p. 124.

instruction) are ex-officio. Here a set of politically determined offices are dominated numerically by governmental representatives. The interest groups in education include the NEA-affiliated Illinois Education Association, the Illinois Agricultural Association, the State Association of School Boards, the Chicago Board of Education, and sometimes the Chamber of Commerce. However great the power of educational association leaders may be toward influencing and dominating the commission, the basic structural characteristics of the linkage are state-wide in nature. One would have difficulty arguing that chambers of commerce and agricultural associations are captured and coopted by educationists. Furthermore, the numerical strength lies in the hands of legislators; therefore, even if the SPC has been heavily influenced and near capture by the Illinois educationist group, as Masters *et al.* seem to indicate, the structural link must be treated as a type of its own government rather than extra-governmental in character. Thus, the structure is the focal point of component units of state-wide educational interest groups, governmentally brought together, with representatives who are governmental officials in their commission roles originating from independent organizations. They are a coalition. This form is called ***state-wide syndical.***

Correlates of Structural Types

With some knowledge concerning the types of linkage structure, it is possible to hypothesize certain correlates of structure for further research. For example, if certain specifiable differences exist among states hypothesized as related to their type of politics of education (defined by the patterns found at their respective points of tangency between the legislature and the educational interest groups), then, once a state is identified by its type, correlates of type can be examined to see if the hypothesized relationships exist. Because action in life must often be taken without full knowledge of the situation, knowing the relationship between structural type and other aspects of one's state increases a group's chances to influence policy making in the politics of education. At least, it may suggest where *not* to put one's energy.

Any discussion of classification systems should provide categories which are mutually exclusive and which exhaust the universe under consideration. The latter goal is easier to achieve if the universe for the task consists in the published reports cited earlier. Otherwise, this task falls short of its exhaustive goal. The author will not offer categories that are mutually exclusive because that ideal is only attainable at the sacrifice of categories which seem worth noting. For example, a category of political life style picks out a characteristic flavor of political behavior from each type of state. Allocation of types of state politics on the classic *Gemeinschaft-*

Gesellschaft continuum overlaps political life style. One is much more global, having value for students and researchers, while the other is more specific to behavior, selecting a few aspects for attention. It seems wiser here to risk breaking down walls between some categories than to lose them altogether.

Hypotheses may be offered concerning the role which the points of tangency of the four types are likely to play in educational legislation. The probable power of the education lobby in each type of state may be assessed in relation to each role and each structural type. Hypotheses may also be offered concerning the legislature in each type. Aspects of the legislative process, exclusive of the pressure group operations outside its walls, will be used to illustrate the possibilities. (1) Where does the process accommodation of interests, necessary for the passage of educational legislation, take place? (2) What are the sentiments and attitudes of legislators toward education people in each type, and how do they view school people? (3) In what types of states are education people most successful with legislatures, and where do they characteristically initiate or oppose legislation?

Before answering these questions, the author warns students who may demand a mathematical derivation from premise to conclusion for the flow from theory to hypotheses that the course taken here is not the mathematic-deductive one of Herbert Fiegel.[27] Instead, the author's knowledge from reading about the phenomenological universe has invaded the neat reasoning. This analysis is *post factum* because: (1) the data were conceived, collected, and communicated to the field by an atheoretical method; (2) long discussions with graduate students touched briefly the basic ideas involved; and (3) the author prefers interacting with people in complex social systems as a basis for theory construction. The "logic" here may often be a rationalization of the data; such hypotheses do have value.

Where is the chief locus of accommodation likely to be in each of the four types? The answer is implicit in the nature of the social structure, if a specific structural type can account for the interaction patterns of the groups involved in educational legislation. Consider Type I *(locally-based disparate):* the likelihood of accommodation is low among the geographically-separated units of school districts where local pride dominates the behavior. The focus of accommodation on educational legislation in such locally-based disparate states will be *inside* the legislature, probably on the floor of each house. With Type II *(state-wide monolithic),* the accommodation of interests takes place outside the legislature but inside

[27] Herbert Feigl, "Principles and Problems of Theory Construction," in *Current Trends in Psychological Theory* (Pittsburgh, University of Pittsburgh Press, 1951), p. 182.

the monolith. The monolith's tasks will get legislation through the houses without upsetting the prior accommodation. Type III *(state-wide fragmented)* faces problems similar to Type I, for it must fight inside the legislature unless various educational interests work together (then the term "fragmented" would hardly apply). Finally, Type IV *(state-wide syndical)* will find an accommodation inside its operations. The existence of governmental members virtually insures such accommodation. This function is given to the point of tangency between the legislature and educational interests.

What are the sentiments and attitudes of legislators toward education people in each type? How do they view school people? Based on the thesis that difficulties lead to frustration, frustration to anger, and anger, in turn is directed against the perceived causes of frustration; and based on another thesis that one is often led to feel great respect for a person (especially in vote counting) if one experiences that person's power; it is possible to generalize about sentiments and concepts. In this manner, legislator sentiment toward education and education's spokesmen, and legislators' views of school people can be considered in each of the four types of states.

In the case of Type I states, *locally-based disparate* linkage structures appear automatically to involve the status of key spokesmen, which is clearly higher than the rank and file teacher status. The dominant local-view-of-the-world reinforces the notion that teachers are paternalistically controllable and that key superintendents will be respected and heeded on educational matters by legislators, particularly those nearest the chief schoolmen.

In the case of Type II states, *state-wide monolithic* linkage structures appear to legislators to represent the totality of the profession in their state. The monolithic structure resulting in a united front suggests that teachers are *a single public* rather than several publics within teaching. The warm sentiment evoked by "Mr. Chips" and the school marm in American folklore is extended to all members of the pyramid, weakening the opposition—even the fumbling weakness of the superintendent in *The Child Buyer* [28] lays the legislator open to seductive cooptation. Legislators will respond to this type of linkage as most people, including college undergraduates, do. Educationists seen as a total group will be viewed positively as very high in social service and activity, but low in power.[29]

In the case of Type III states, *state-wide fragmented* linkage structures display components approaching the legislative hearings arguing among themselves all the way. The distinctions among education's insiders—teachers and administrators, board members, and competing teacher groups—are highly visible to legislators who are often forced to take sides,

---

[28] John Hershey, *The Child Buyer* (New York: Alfred A. Knopf, Inc., 1960).

[29] Donald D. O'Dowd and David C. Beardsley, "Student Image of the School Teacher," *Phi Delta Kappan, XXXXII,* (March, 1961), pp. 250–254.

thereby gaining kudos from some constituents and censure from others. Hostility toward some education groups is likely to result. In addition, a picture emerges of good and bad persons in education. Usually the "school administrator establishment hierarchy" is seen as the "bad guys" and the "poor classroom teacher" as the "good guys." The frustration which legislators must develop at their inability to find real agreement among educationists should hurt educational causes seriously; legislative stalemates could result if Type III states were not openly engaged in extensive public debate actually resulting in higher political gain for legislators acting on educational matters. This more active public interest in Type III states certainly tends to generate greater awareness of the political power of schoolmen even with fragmented association networks, and it means a greater respect by legislators for that power.

In the case of Type IV states, *state-wide syndical* linkage structures are likely to find educationists more positively valued by legislators. The continuous interaction between members of the legislature and the educational interest groups, represented on the governmental unit involved, tends to reinforce the peer relation implied with membership inside this agency. The minimal conflict on the floor (and even in committee) over many educational matters resulting from the "legislative-council" approach could simplify the legislator's task. Any governmental linkage agency, such as the Illinois School Problems Commission, would probably gain prestige. Legislators would consider it truly expert and its direction worth following. Thus, the agency would be attributed with even greater power than it actually has because of the following factors: (1) Legislators need a "fall guy." When an agency appears untouchable and above partisan strife, legislators can blame that agency for their own failure to comply with constituents' demands. "It's no use if *they* (the agency) won't approve it" becomes a convenient excuse to pigeonhole constituents' requests which seem foolish, harmful, or uninteresting to the legislator. Thus, positive sentiments toward education and its representatives will characterize Type IV as well as Type II states. (2) The attributed power, especially to the key linkage component, tends to be greater in Type IV states. The fact may not fit the attribution because the apex of Type II structural units results from a united pyramid and cooptation, while Type IV's unity is more likely to reflect bargaining among its component elements. The presence of legislators in this, however, tends to make it difficult for coalition members to move around it.

In what types of states are education people most successful with legislatures, and where do they characteristically initiate or oppose legislation? Lobbies are effective when they prevent legislation which is contrary to the interests they represent or when they secure legislation which furthers their interests. It is usually easier to prevent legislation than to pass it.

Thus, a lobby with influence in the executive office might secure a veto of legislation it disapproves of, although it might lack the capacity to get a bill out of committee or through either house. Again, a lobby may concentrate its resources on a given committee in order to have it pigeonhole a measure, thus avoiding a vote on the floor. For much proposed legislation, sufficient influence to swing one legislative committee of either house is enough to prevent passage. Moving a bill through its rites of passage is frequently another matter requiring different strategies and much more influence. The relative power of lobbies becomes apparent in the distinction between the power to prevent or the power to secure passage of laws. In effect, the first question is: "Can the organized educational professionals prevent hostile legislation?" The next question is: "Can they secure the passage of bills they initiate?" At first glance, the number of bills opposed and espoused successfully, compared to those opposed and supported unsuccessfully, appears to be an over-simplified merging of equal numbers for each legislative item without discriminating for their significance. One cannot ignore the possibility that a law opposed unsuccessfully, e. g., a proposal revolutionizing the ground rules for entrance into the profession, may have more to tell about the lack of legislative influence of an education lobby than any number of successful bills supported through the same session. It is more difficult to estimate what a lobby has avoided because it felt insufficiently influential to gain more. Here is a subtle and significant factor so difficult to compare that it seems nearly impossible. On the other hand, two factors facilitate judgments concerning the relative influence of education lobbies in one state as compared with another. If the typology does deal with truly significant differences in the type of educational politics of a state, then the variation between two types is likely to be large enough to judge. Furthermore, there are fifty states, not eleven. When data is gathered on more cases of each type, the central tendency for each type, if there is one, will become clearer. Now we are dealing with data comparing only eleven states.

Even within the limits of the eleven cases reported, certain things become clear. The *locally-based disparate* Type I states have not fared well in passing legislation although they seem successful in preventing legislation.[30] This is logically consistent with the nature of the type. Taking into account the capacity of the profession to obtain state aid, legislation strengthens this judgment.[31] Thus, Type I states may be classified as having the power to prevent but not to pass legislation.

State-wide monolithic Type II states also display the capacity to prevent legislation.[32] In addition, they have proud records of initiating education

[30] Bailey *et al.*, pp. 92–102.
[31] *Ibid.*
[32] Masters *et al.*, pp. 12–98.

law successfully. In New York, the epitome of the type, the education lobby has been considered the strongest in the state. The question, "Is the 'box score' as good as it appears because of the power of the lobby or because of the nature of the politics of education?" is a doubt raised by the Masters report on Missouri. By graphic example, a wary football coach knows that he can impress the alumni by picking opponents who look good because of past prestige or performance but who are not too strong this year; if he is measured by the win-loss column, he will turn in a great record. The educational lobby of Type II states resembles such intelligent coaches at times. No one seeks the toughest battles in the legislative process whatever his sporting instincts are. The game is played for the stakes involved. Furthermore, Type II states have a monolithic educational-interest structure. This is the familiar structure of Butler and Carroll G. Pearse, described by its preferred internal politics: closed system consensus (*see* Chapter 2). As a way of life and a technique of organizational struggle, the group avoids open conflict. Thus, the sub-cultural drives, the stakes involved, the appearance of power to be lost or won all seem to compress the lobby and limit its goals. Its box score of legislative bills won and lost may be misleading. Nevertheless, the educational organizations in this type certainly have more influence over legislation than in the first. They can prevent legislation, pass a great many bills, and traditionally lead the way in acquiring monies for education.

State-wide fragmented Type III politics of education appear to have less powerful education lobbies than Type I cases; some data would argue this, but the overall data are conflicting. Here the paucity of present research is obvious. Against the weakness of fragmentation must be laid the intensity of open conflict that draws such organizations as the AFL-CIO in Michigan [33] into the educational battles; otherwise these organizations would never have been involved. The process mobilizes social power from far-flung networks not usually participating in the legislative process resulting in education law in Type II states. In any case, the structural nature of the key links between educational organizations and the legislature virtually dictates that some educational groups will be successful in their support of certain legislation, each winning and losing some battles but openly fighting in all battles. The financial data on Michigan, compared with Type II states, is much better than one might expect.[34] The lobby here must be classified as mixed toward preventing and passing legislation. If measured by its successes in representing members or clients, as the clients seem to express themselves, it is less influential than Type II lobbies. If measured by the successful yield to educational welfare, although not necessarily expressed by the schools and teachers, the lobby *is more effec-*

[33] Masters *et al.*

[34] *Ibid.*

tive. Visible politics may be better for all concerned and more effective in expressing the true will of the people than invisible politics with more influence.[35]

The education lobby's power in *state-wide syndical* Type IV structures is surely greater than in Type I states. The need for bargaining agreements militates power in opposite directions when it comes to passing laws. The general power to prevent hostile legislation flows logically from the nature of the long-term close association and warm sentiments which are likely to result in this point of tangency. The probable cost in limiting goals after bargaining is less sure, but there must be costs in this process. More important would be the question: "Who has a chair at the table?" The Illinois case does not explore the potential limits and boundaries of the structure now composed of relatively unaggressive associational members. In any case, one essential result of coalition and bargaining is a limitation of yield comparable to accepting half a loaf in lieu of none. Thus, Type IV structures may be classified as able to prevent hostile legislation, able to pass legislation it agrees upon, but likely to undershoot its immediate potential gains for a long-term relationship. Here it is akin to Type II states. If Type IV structures do reflect the publics inside the educational interest group complex, because of its coalitional bargaining rather than monolithic consensus, it is, however likely to undershoot as far as Type II structures do.

The typology and its correlation of legislative efforts, including the lobby's hypothesized power to prevent and to pass legislation, the sentiments of legislators, and the typical loci of accommodation are summarized in Figure 2.

Since the key linkage structures with their patterns of intersection mediate between legislature and interest group, the implications of particular structures and patterns are likely to be greater for the association networks tied to the legislative process than for the legislature. Although it may "call the tune" at times in certain states, *the lobby exists because of the legislature,* not the other way around! The correlates of structural type which may be hypothesized from the association network of educational interest groups are tied to the key link with the legislature and legislation. Relevant information for legislative decision making is obviously very valuable. The role played by expertise to provide prestige, peer recognition, and high informal status among legislators is cherished for its information and understanding. No one is generally expert on all legislative matters. Thus, to executive branch bureaucrats and to lobbyists information becomes an almost incalculable premium toward legislative influence, putting legis-

---

[35] Stephen K. Bailey *et al., Schoolmen and Politics* (Syracuse, N.Y.: Syracuse University Press, 1962), p. X.

LEGISLATIVE RELATIONSHIPS

Structure of Key Link / Correlates	I DISPARATE (Locally-based)	II MONOLITHIC (State-wide)	III FRAGMENTED (State-wide)	IV SYNDICAL (State-wide)
LOBBY POWER:				
Prevention	Yes	Yes	Mixed Yes and No	Yes
Initiation	No	Yes	Mixed Yes and No	Yes
LEGISLATOR SENTIMENT	Warm & Paternal to Teachers	Warm, undifferentiated	Differentiated: Critical to Administrators; Warm to Teachers	Warm, not Critical
LOCUS OF ACCOMMODATION	Legislature	Apex of Monolith	Legislature	The Group of Syndics

Figure 2. Typology of linkage structures correlated to legislative effects and appraisal.

lators in one another's debt. A well-run lobby can make an "expert" legislator.

At this moment in the political history of education's changing power structure, it is relevant and timely to examine several points: (1) the variations in the existence and control of information correlated with structural type; (2) the customary political life style of the educational organizations and their members, especially those models of behavior, the organizational elites; (3) the nature of the educationist elites heading each type and located at the chief linkages to the legislature; and (4) that ubiquitous German continuum of *Gemeinschaft-Gesellschaft* which Howard Becker [36] translated and transmuted as the sacred-secular continuum.[36]

The relationship frequently seen between American ruralism and localism, as well as the arrested development of education into the twentieth century, suggests that Type I *disparate* state educational interest structures will display a dominance of *gemeinschaftlich* in contrast to *gesellschaftlich* educational beliefs, knowledge, outlook, and sense of community. Type II *monolithic* structures will be somewhat closer to the *Gesellschaft* end of the continuum than the *disparate* but still essentially *Gemeinschaft* in beliefs, etc. With the Type III *fragmented* structures, instead, secularization is found; the educational outlook, beliefs, knowledge and sense of association are clearly *Gesellschaft*. Type IV *syndical* structures are again more likely to produce *gemeinschaftlich* outlooks and beliefs. However, the nature of the associations participating will heavily influence the result, and *some of the patterns of consensus* (most likely the politics of the priestcraft) *will reproduce the aura of the sacred community,* primarily because an accommodation had to be reached under the eyes of the legislators! The *syndical* structure will not go as far toward the secular as will the *fragmented* type.

Thus, hypothesizing the characteristic verbal expression and the organizational preference exhibited by participants of educational interest groups, we can rank the four types of political structures along a *Gemeinschaft-Gesellschaft* continuum with no attempt at equal interval scaling. Type I and Type II will be very high and high, respectively, toward the *Gemeinschaft*. Type IV will blend midway between the terminals, and Type III will be nearest the *Gesellschaft* terminal (see Figure 3).

Further substantiation of the positions of the *disparate, monolithic,* and *fragmented* types allocated on this continuum is the work of Seymour Evans at New York University.[37] Evans studied the organization of schools in relation to bureaucratic theory and found that the predisposition of teachers, along a *Gemeinschaft-Gesellschaft* continuum, was related to their

---

[36] Howard Becker, *Systematic Sociology* (New York: John Wiley & Sons, 1932), pp. 223–226.

[37] Seymour Evans, "Toward a Theory of Teacher Collective Organizational Behavior" (Unpublished doctoral dissertation, New York University, 1966).

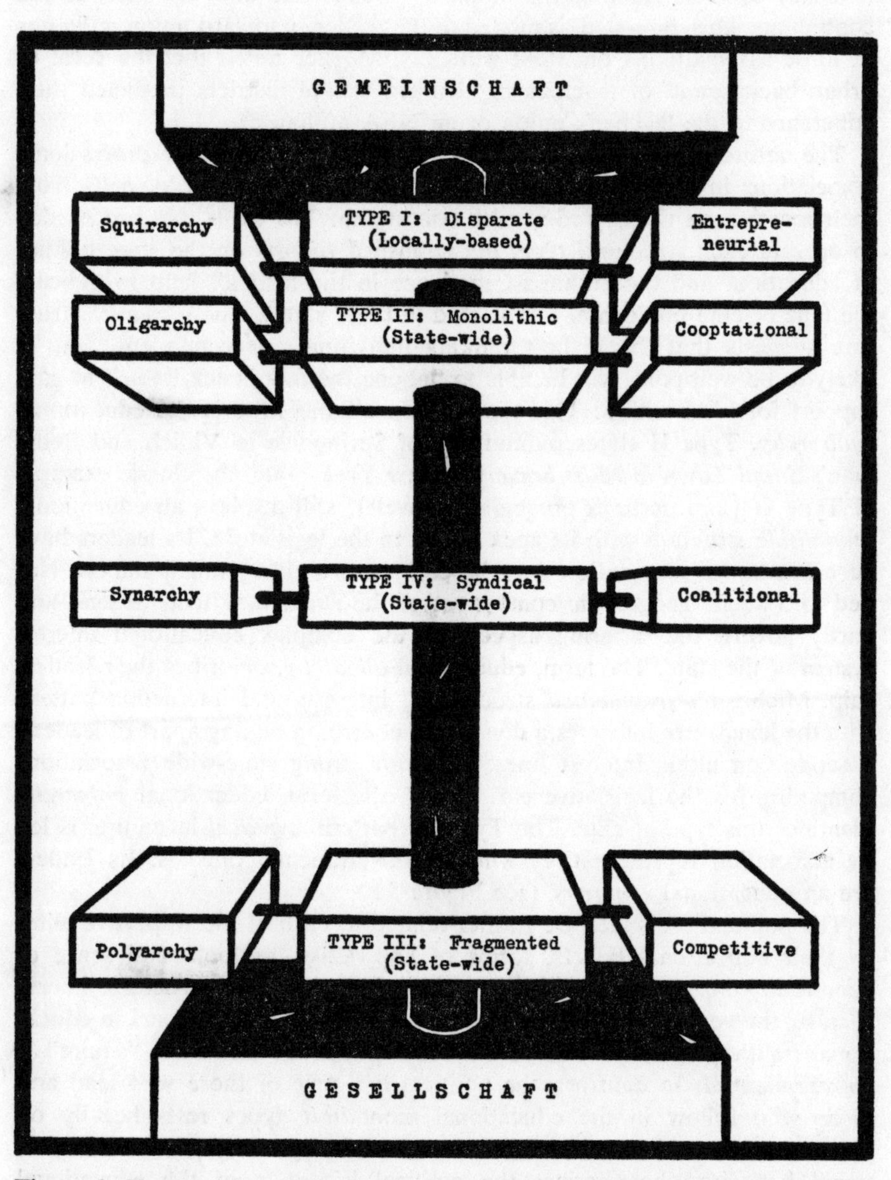

Figure 3. Types of key links in the State Politics of Education correlated to Political Life Styles and Elites ranked along the Gemeinschaft-Gesellschaft continuum. (This Area is represented in Sec. A, Fig. 1)

tendency to seek organization along a bureaucratic and pre-bureaucratic continuum. This, he noted, is related to the tendency toward union militancy or loose association. Consistent with this, Moeller noted that the rural or urban background of teachers in identical school districts predicted their adherence to the teacher's union or an NEA affiliate.[38]

The nature of the educationist elite, found at the top of the professional associations in the states of each type, follow partially and logically from their location on the sacred-secular continuum. The skills that are needed to operate each structural type, the published reports on the state politics of education, and the author's experience in the field all help to indicate the type of elite one can expect to find in these states. The *disparate* structure suggests that the highest ranking individual superintendent, who is likely to be well paid, will be able to "phone the folks back home" to gain support for his position. This type of educationist elite is the educational *squirarchy*. Type II states remind one of Springdale in Vidich and Bensman's *Small Town in Mass Society*.[39] New York State, the classic example of Type II (and perhaps progenitor as well), still displays an educational *monolithic* structure with its apex linked to the legislature. Its leaders have been masters of cooptation and the consensus-building manipulation. Not tied to a single geographic component of the state, they tend to lead and partly govern the differing aspects of the complex educational interest system of the state. The term, educational *oligarchy,* describes their leadership. Michigan's *fragmented* structure of interests and interaction pattern with the legislature indicates a division of control, a pulling apart of leaders, a separation along interest lines, but with strong state-wide associations competing for the legislative ear. Hence, the term, educational *polyarchy* identifies this type of elite. The Type IV pattern, *syndical* in nature, is led by association representatives who are governmental officials. Its leaders are an educational *synarchy* (see Figure 3).

The political life styles are further related to each of the respective elites by their educational beliefs, forms of knowledge, outlook, and sense of community that are characteristic of each type of political structure. Therefore, by the very methods these leaders use in dealing with others in educational politics, the behavioral characteristic of the educational "squire" is *entrepreneurial*. In contrast, the political life style of those who lead and those who follow in the educational *monolithic* types rests heavily on persuasion, on the search for agreement, and finally on cooptation. Cooptational behavior characterizes the political life style of the educational *oligarchs,* the educationist elite in the type occurring most frequently. The

---

[38] Gerald H. Moeller, "The Relationship between Bureaucracy in School System Organization and Teachers," (Unpublished doctoral dissertation, Washington University, 1962).

[39] Vidich and Bensman.

polyarchy of Type III states engages in political behavior and displays a life style most familiar to those for whom two-party struggles are a normal way of life. Secularized and tougher, in fact, than the *oligarchy* of Type II states, the political life style of this group is *competitive* throughout the realm of their associational networks. *Coalitional* behavior characterizes the life style natural to the *synarchy,* with the recognition of identifiable spheres of influence accorded each group.

The *Gemeinschaft-Gesellschaft* continuum may be used to arrange the organizational types of structure found in the key point of tangency linking the legislature to the networks of educationists and correlates of these types (see Figure 3).

The control of information and its quantity at points of access to the legislative process are extremely important sources of influence in the modern legislature. By having data on this dimension alone, a researcher who had no other might pinpoint more accurately the sources of influence over the sources of legislation than he would with any other data. Again, untidy as the sacred-secular continuum is, it too is related, conceptually and phenomenologically, to the nature and control of information.

The *disparate* type of structure with the leadership of the educational squires is short of information. Because of the individualistic, entrepreneurial, localist short-sightedness of its leaders, who laud practical "horse sense" about education when they can actually evaluate a horse's points for county fairs far better than a school program, this structure relies upon folklore and myth in education for its information. The little information it has is scattered and cannot be brought to bear effectively upon the legislative process with respect to education. Quite different are matters regarding quantity, nature, and control of information in the *monolithic* state. The *monolothic* nature of the interest structure itself indicates the *oligarchy's* capacity to deliver what information it has quickly, pinpointed to a target, and specific in detail to influence the legislative process. The *monolith* has a virtual monopoly of information and, as a result, the legislature is conditioned to depend on the *monolith* for its data. The amount and sophistication of these data are high, limited only by the conceptual frameworks of the "scribblers" who historically developed the categories of information and used the theories underlying their use. (Here is the customary vulnerability of closed systems—rigid and repetitive behavior even when no longer appropriate.) To all intents and purposes, the data at hand indicate no significant difference between Type II and Type IV structures regarding the quantity, nature, and control of data that each has. Type III states are another matter. Here more information exists than is characteristically present in Type II states. Moreover, it exists in various forms, not all of which fit the conceptual frameworks of the educationist "scribblers." Other "scribblers" may help determine the flow of information into the legislative process where it functions competitively to pull the legislator this way and that way. This is depicted diagrammatically in Figure 4.

Summary

The politics of education at the state level consists of four basic types of structure, depending upon the nature of the characteristic patterns of interaction taking place at points of tangency which link the legislature and the network of educational interest groups in the particular state. The organizational structure of these key points of tangency was first used to provide indicators of the types that have been described in the published reports by Stephen Bailey *et al.,* Nicholas Masters *et al.,* and Michael Usdan on New England, New Jersey, New York, Illinois, Michigan, and Missouri, cited earlier. Then it was possible to identify elements related to the legislative process in educational matters and, in turn, relate these to each organizational structural type of link between the legislature and the educational interests. These correlates include the characteristic locus of accommodation about educational law, the expressed sentiments of legislators combined with their view of education's legislative spokesmen and the profession as a whole. Indeed, the extent to which the profession is seen "as a whole" was one variable in this discussion. Finally, the probability of the education lobby actually influencing the legislature became another variable related to the four types of states in the politics of education.

In a similar manner, correlates of each of the four types of organizational links were identified by "turning one's back" to the legislature—toward the associational network of interest groups tied through each linkage pattern to the legislature. The quantity, nature, and control of information characteristically available to each linkage type was noted. The educational sub-culture most consistent with the data from the eleven states and logically consistent with linkage type was used to locate the four types on the sacred-secular continuum. Similarly, the characteristic political behavior of each type—the political life style—was noted and charted. The educationist ruling elite typically found in each organizational type was noted. The whole study produces a taxonomy on the state politics of education. (See Figure 1.)

Again, remember that the empirical bases for the illustrated taxonomy consist in the reports on eleven states only, which is a limiting factor. These reports also indicate that more cases of Type II states exist than any other. This makes sense in several ways. The *monolithic* form fits the politics preferred by pedagogues. It is the closest to informal closed-system politics; unlike the *syndical* form, it does not include elected officials. Also, its form was heavily influenced by the schoolmen "scribblers," such as Paul Mort and his protégés. One would expect to find this as the prevailing pattern.

Organizational Link / Correlates	TYPE I DISPARATE	TYPE II MONOLITHIC	TYPE IV SYNDICAL	TYPE III FRAGMENTED
INFORMATION:				
Quantity	Small	Large	Large	Very large
Nature	Unscientific	Precise and Predictable	Precise and Predictable	Scientific, but not Predictable
Control	Personalistic (Little)	Monopolistic	Monopolistic	Competitive

Figure 4. Types of linkage structures correlated to the Quantity, Nature, and Control of Information. (This Area is represented in Sec. B, Fig. 1)

CHAPTER 4

The Changing State Politics of Education

The influence of the politics of education on governing and, hence, on the policies of education is the central concern of this book. The issue of the mutability of public education in the United States may, indeed, be the single most important educational question Americans will have to answer in this decade. On the one hand, demands for educational reform are increasing; on the other, the closed-system tendencies of educationist power structures and the filibuster tactics of pedagogical spokesmen and lobbyists blunt the thrust of educational reforms. This frustrating non-confrontation is likely to produce an unnecessary revision of the constitutional arrangements for governing education. Unfortunately, as with most educational changes this mid-century, the revisions would add little to the classroom learning of pupils.

The dominant pattern of educational state politics will be described in detail. The published research of state educational politics will be reviewed with questions concerning change and basic political readjustment of the state politics of education. A developmental construct will be offered to describe the pattern of change characteristically present in the state politics of education. Finally, a judgment on the viability of present constitutional arrangements will be offered.

The Dominant Pattern

New York, Missouri, and New Jersey will be used to illustrate details of the dominant pattern. New York and Missouri may be valuable for another reason: if Missouri's pyramid is as informal as the monolithic linkage structure can become, then New York's pyramid is as formal.

The schoolmen's pyramid of state-wide associations in Missouri is topped by Executive Secretary Everett Keith of the Missouri State Teachers Association. The "Princeton Group" functions as New Jersey's citadel agency linked through customary patterns of interaction: the education association (and NEA affiliate), the state education department, and the state school board association. In Type II states, the department of education tends to be captured, coopted, and controlled by the monolith. New York State offers a case of the monolithic type in all its beautiful symmetry; the New York State Education Conference Board is the monolith's citadel agency and the key link to the legislature.

In Type II states, the state school board plays a quiescent role, registering the proposals of the chief state school officer. In these states, the state education department, interlocking with the citadel agency at the apex of the association pyramid, seldom provides leadership for the state. This does not imply that members of the department may not be included as members of the citadel agency. The point is that the state department does not automatically stand above other educational interest groups in the extra-legal apex, linking the interest groups to the legislature even though membership in this apex unit is customary. The state school board members play an inactive "buffer" role without a bridge to the legislature.

The most significant and powerful roles in these monolithic pyramids are played by school administrators, appearing in various organizational roles. They often appear directly as representatives of school administrator associations within the monolith. They also appear less overtly, but no less powerfully, as incumbents of offices of school people other than administrators. Thus, characteristically, especially in Type II states, the executive secretary of the state teachers association will be a former school administrator. Similarly, the policy board and career offices of the state school board association will include former school superintendents, who often dominate the association. Department of education personnel included in the citadel agency are usually former school administrators. The pattern of overwhelming administrator dominance is not an "establishment conspiracy."

The recent teacher militancy reflects gains made by the American Federation of Teachers and the classroom teachers associations of the National Education Association. For the AFT, membership of school administration in teacher organizations is a crucial issue; to the federation, inclusion of supervisors in the same organization with those supervised results in control of the organization by the supervisors. An analysis of NEA groups throughout most of this century supports their position. But such positions only reflect the past. The United Federation of Teachers' victory in New York City is evidence of a position shift, as are the changes in the behavior of the NEA classroom teachers groups. It would be an oversimplification to accept either the AFT view of the NEA "administrator-dominated" power structure or the NEA view of labor-dominated AFT. In both cases, as the size of membership has increased and as the internal bureaucracies developed, the tendency has been for the associational and organizational careerists to dominate their respective associations. Therefore, former school administrators occupy citadel agency posts as representatives of a range of educational interests. They still represent a point of view which must be considered the school administrator's. Consequently, the views of top-echelon men will be predictably more like those of school administrators than like those of teachers.

To what extent are teacher interests represented to the legislature in the dominant type of state? There are several ways of asking this question to indicate its importance to teachers. For example: What types of legislation have priority from those who occupy the citadel agency position? Does curriculum become a matter of concern? Is classroom size or equalization in financial matters a problem of legislative priority? The legislative record has been clear during this century. The dominant type in the state politics of education has resulted in legislation for three areas of education, all major concerns to professors ("scribblers") of school administration and superintendents. These are legislation for: (1) financing of schools, (2) reorganization of school districts, and (3) certification of educational personnel. Administrators or students of school administration will argue that these were and are the real issues for legislation. Legislation providing for teacher negotiation is largely the product of developments in Type III states (Michigan and California). The resulting verdict seems clear from several approaches. There is less than adequate teacher representation *among office holders in associations that are "supposed" to represent teachers* in the citadel agency of the monolithic type. Cooptation of teacher groups partly explains the lack of representation. Administrator domination is the political life style preferred by pedagogues in Type II states.

What is true of teacher representation is generally true of school board association and lay group representation. Cooptation has resulted in overrepresentation of school administration interests and outlooks within PTA and school board groups as well as teacher groups. If one set of interests and point of view were to be maximized, the author, committed to the belief in the centrality of school administration to the educational venture, would argue for this set. Much of the evidence available clearly indicates that the school administrator view has been traditionally maximized. Is the maximization of one educational interest at the expense of others necessary or wise? A close examination of the membership of the organizational linkage between associations and the legislature in New York State indicates the extent to which the dominant organizational pattern is monolithic and likely to be monopolistic, with power to influence legislation in that state as well.

The New York State Educational Conference Board is one of the most carefully constructed and well-established apex linkage units in any Type II state. The Conference Board's record of achievements in producing educational legislation and influencing the state legislature is the envy of other lobbies in the state. In addition, New York's Conference Board has provided a model for other states. The formalization of roles of educational interests, included at this level of the monolith, has advanced further in New York than in most states; the contrast with Missouri, another Type II state, illustrates this point. Finally, more published data on New York's education lobby are available than on any other state of this type.

The Conference Board consists of nine members: four chairs are held by administrator groups (two superintendent groups and the elementary and secondary principals associations); the fifth chair, the school board association (whose secretary is a former school administrator); the sixth chair, the New York State Congress of Parents and Teachers;[1] the seventh chair, the New York Citizen's Committee for the Public Schools;[2] the eighth chair, the New York State Teachers Association, and NEA affiliate;[3] the ninth chair, the Public Education Association of New York City (this interest offers the city's schools a chance to surmount and so survive current problems as an urban counterpart of the New York State Citizens Committee; the PEA alone represents the city on the Conference Board).

In virtually every state where the urban-rural division of interests is seen, the issues of geographic representation tend to be issues of the balance between rural and urban power. The PEA as a loyal opposition becomes even more significant when one realizes that each of the other eight associations are effectively apportioned against the urban interests. Rural dominance, extending to the internal power structures of the apex's component associations, is the rule of Type II monolithic states. Thus, the Type II organizational apex, linking the legislature with educational interests groups, produces a united front on educational legislation. This unity results from cooptation of member associations, such as teachers, parents, and board members, by organizational leaders with school administration orientation. City educational interest groups are further coopted by rural leaders, i.e., rural in characteristic nostalgia and values committed to the sacred community. Indeed, cooptation is the behavioral pattern within the monolith, constituting the usual political life style. This characteristic is beyond dispute when the Conference Board is, itself, placed in perspective. "In reality, however, the Conference Board is a sounding board for and a refiner of the deliberations of an inner core of seven schoolmen."[4] These

---

1 PTA's are usually coopted organizations lacking independent information gathering resources. Similarly, at the local level Vidich and Bensman's description of the manipulation of the PTA by the supervising principal in Springdale agrees with the author's experience as professor of education *and* suburban parent. Arthur J. Vidich and Joseph Bensman, *Small Town in Mass Society* (Garden City, N.Y.: Doubleday & Company, Inc., 1960), pp 193–199.

2 This organization's membership is gerrymandered against the urban centers. Laurence Iannaccone, "Future of State Politics of Education," in Frank W. Lutz and Joseph J. Azzarelli eds., *Struggle for Power in Education* (New York: The Center for Applied Research in Education, Inc., 1966), p. 53.

3 The NYSTA is the only teacher association in the apex of the monolith. It too is gerrymandered against the urban centers and its offices are largely staffed by school administrators not teachers.

4 Stephen K. Bailey *et al., Schoolmen in Politics* (Syracuse: Syracuse University Press, 1962), p. 36.

men are masters of cooptation and the "norm" setters of the type.

Organizations within the monolithic apex unit normally include the state department of education. Officially, this is absent in the New York case. Other Type II states do not operate with their monolith's citadel agency so exposed to public view and as formally as New York State: the state education department was a member of California's apex prior to Governor Edmund Brown's tenure; it is still found in the Missouri structure; it is formally present in the "Princeton Group" in New Jersey; however, it appears only through the "inner core of seven schoolmen" in New York. Two of the seven schoolmen, reported by Stephen Bailey and his team,[5] were members of the state education department. Michael Usdan's report documented (with pride in the political acumen of schoolmen) how difficult it was for participants to draw any distinction between those who were staff members of the Conference Board and those who were members of the state education department; the New York State Commissioner of Education wrote a letter resolving this distinction.[6] The inner seven were secretaries and research arms of the Conference Board's key components. Chief architect, major strategist, and tactical commander of the seven was Paul Mort, until his death in May, 1962; through the inner core, he also led the Conference Board.[7] Again, the sacred-rural values expressed by Mort, even the prose imagery of his writing, appeared in the genesis of the Conference Board. Mort's model was the New York State Conference Board of Farm Organizations.[8]

Summarily, a majority of the eleven states recently studied display patterns of interaction in an organizational unit linking the interest groups to the legislature. The organizational unit is the chief link between the legislature and the educational interests; it is the keystone of the pyramid of organizations working together to influence legislation. The system is an organizational monolith, politically monopolistic with regard to professional influence over educational legislation. The monolith is presided over by school administrators and ex-school administrators. Included within the monolith are components coopted from school board, teacher, and lay citizen associations. No teachers' group excluding school administrator members appears in the apex of this pyramid; however, administrator associations, not open to teachers, are represented. The urban centers are heavily under-represented. The rural emphasis reinforces the *Gemeinschaft* concept—the sacred-community orientations—as the dominant pattern of state educational politics. Informal cooptation by key "scribblers" in school

[5] *Ibid.*

[6] Michael Usdan, *The Political Power of Education in New York State* (New York: Institute of Administrative Research, Teachers College, Columbia University, 1963), p. 37.

[7] Bailey, pp. 36–37.

[8] *Ibid.*, p. 37.

administration occurs, as well as formal cooptation of various component associations. Hence, the pyramid is ruled by an educational oligarchy whose political life style is cooptational.

The characteristic activity pattern displayed by the pyramid may be separated into three phases: (1) formulating a legislative program; (2) marshalling information to influence the legislative process; and (3) mobilizing power to influence legislator voting. These phases are not as phenomenologically discrete as they are conceptually discrete. In particular, marshalling information and mobilizing support to influence legislators overlap, reinforce, and, on occasion, merge to become the two sides of a coin. Bringing information to bear selectively on an issue becomes a form of influence upon legislator voting behavior.

Formulating a legislative program generally precedes the legislative session. In New York State, Mort and the other finance experts, the educational administration "scribblers," played a particularly prominent role in this phase. The establishment of a legislative program for the pyramid requires: (1) selection of particular legislative goals, most often financial; (2) collection and organization of information for subsequent use in the legislative process; and (3) solicitation of support from component members of the pyramid. Unlike New York, some states have had to rely upon the importation of "scribbler" consultants to help in this formulation phase when a new basic school-finance formula or a new direction of educational policy, such as developing a master plan for junior colleges, was undertaken.[9]

When the legislative program has been formulated and adopted by the power pyramid apex, the second phase develops: the legislative program is submitted to the legislative process. This usually involves the cooperation of key legislators to sponsor the pyramid's bills. These legislator friends are often perceived by their peers as experts in educational matters as a result of the knowledge they gain and display as a consequence of the continuous exchange between them and the pyramid lobbyists. Their putative expertise tends to be real. It is acquired in frequent interaction with educationist experts, who simultaneously educate, influence, and create the legislator expert. Marshalling information goes beyond getting a bill introduced. The pyramid's legislative lobbyists appear before committees with other associational members, who are usually prestigious, building a case for the program. Research divisions of the pyramid's component associations play the most critical role in this second phase. The teacher association researchers and the state education department experts have often arrived at the same conclusions, independently, when their respective reports are finally presented before committees. The similarity of conclusions is easily understood,

[9] Iannaccone, p. 54.

apart from the cooptational pattern which underlies it. It would be more surprising were they not to agree, when one realizes that in many states (New York, for instance) the various experts were trained by one man and his students, frequently in the same "shop," using the same concepts, categories of information, and techniques for data collection and analysis. It would also be surprising if legislatures did not, in general, follow this marshalling of information clearly mapped out for them, particularly when the monolithic nature of the pyramid tends to give it a monopoly of relevant information.

Overlapping the second phase, the mobilization of grassroots support to influence legislator voting is increasingly important when the legislative process moves out of committee, to the calendar, and then to the floor. New York State is an example again; evidence indicates the general pattern in other Type II states is similar. The rural bias, historically present, but now being modified, gives an advantage to the rural-based organizational structures of the associations making up the pyramid in at least two ways: (1) the seniority system in legislatures tends to favor the stable rural constituency, and (2) local education people, especially key superintendents and local school board association secretaries or other officers, can more easily reach the rural legislators.

Thus, the "scribbler's" role is central to the first phase of the pyramid's legislative activities—the formulation of the legislative programs—guided by professors and other experts in school administration. The monolith's monopoly of information is marshalled by the legislative spokesmen and research chiefs of its component associations. The citadel agency's network of associations, reaching down to its grassroots and using the relationships back home between its regional schoolmen and their legislative representatives, functions to support the apex and influence legislator votes. Hence, it can frequently ignore the big city—its educational needs, its school people, and even its elected representatives—and still win.

Changes in Types of Structure

The dominant pattern of state educational politics has been described as closed-system monolithic in organizational form, cooptational in political life style, and oligarchic in leadership. If, as suggested in Chapter 2, closed-system politics are the politics preferred by pedagogues, then the dominance of Type II patterns at the state level should not be surprising. Furthermore, the political buffer role of state boards and other special legal and extra-legal arrangements governing education at the state level, including the neutralization of urban legislators, may be expected. The ever-narrowing circles of control to a power elite, informal and extra-legal in nature, usually led by a single individual (such as Mort in New York and

Keith in Missouri), may also be expected. In addition, the tendency toward establishing an internal equilibrium, with increasing stability in the governmental dimension of the state's educational policy making, should be observed over a period of time. If the hypothesized relatively-constant rate of change in the societal dimension also takes place, then a widening gap between governmental and societal dimensions will produce a relatively abrupt shift in the governmental restructure through political action. In the case of a large governmental unit, such as a state, relatively longer periods of stability would be found then in smaller units of government, such as a local school district. If the theoretical system proposed in Chapter 1 offers a useful explanation, then political action leading to a relatively abrupt change in political alignments, power distributions, and policies (in educational legislative affairs) should take place. In Type II states, the change should be especially abrupt because of their closed-system tendencies.

The questions implied in the discussion here may be answered with the empirical evidence used as the basis for the preceding discussion and the taxonomy of Chapter 3. Once again the author feels the strengths and weaknesses of using *post factum* data collected by others without the use of theory. The weakness lies in the capacity of the human mind to make sense where no sense exists. The strength lies in the fact that the data are not related to present theory and, particularly, are *not* concerned with the change process.

The reports do shed some light on the question: Do states change from one political type to another over a period of time? It appears that they do, but perhaps in one direction only. This may be a function of limited information; yet it does seem to fit the classical directions of the growth of organizations in the Western World. In any event, the Type I pattern of state educational politics (locally-based disparate) in its early form appears to graduate into the state-wide monolithic form of Type II. Bailey's study indicated this in New Hampshire. The New Hampshire Joint Committee on the Needs of Education, composed of representatives of the major educational associations, chaired by the Executive Secretary of the Association of School Boards, was considered another Conference Board or "Princeton Group" in New Hampshire.[10] The Bailey team said that New Hampshire "*still* ranks with Massachusetts as representative of the states where permanency is not assured."[11] Their discussion of the Massachusetts power struggles indicated how a locally based disparate type of state almost became a state-wide monolithic type.[12] The development of other interests by Cyril Sargent, before the successful institutionalization of the Massa-

---

[10] Bailey, p. 39.
[11] Bailey, p. 39. (Author's italics.)
[12] *Ibid.*, pp. 63–73.

chusetts Council for the Public Schools, may have prevented that state from joining the ranks of the state-wide monolithic states.[13] In any case, the basic story is clear enough to indicate that the direction of change is from locally-based disparate to state-wide monolithic patterns.

Vermont, on the other hand, was described by the Bailey team as having "a longer . . . row to hoe"; its present disparate structure is illustrated in their report of the struggle over the 1961 finance legislation.[14] While limited, the evidence now indicates: if locally-based disparate states undergo a major revision of their customary entrepreneurial policy-making pattern, they will become state-wide monolithic in structure with the cooptational life style of politics. An examination of the descriptions of state-wide monolithic cases suggests they were once locally-based disparate.[15]

Similarly, the strong state-wide, but fragmented, structural pattern would seem to come after the monolithic one. It may be hypothesized that the existence of a state-wide monolithic pattern is a necessary, though not sufficient, cause to produce a state-wide fragmented pattern. This seems to have been the case in Michigan where "there is no established process . . . to eliminate or modify the factors that cause conflict over education issues. [The first element, which Master *et al.* reported as characteristic of Michigan, implies the transition from the state-wide monolithic types:] First, the education groups that make demands on the legislature are *no longer* unified." [16] In contrasting Michigan—a state-wide fragmented structure of education groups—with the state-wide monolithic structure of Missouri and the syndical structure of Illinois, Masters *et al.* indicated:

> Perhaps the key to understanding the role of education interests in this state is a recognition of the following two points. (1) To a much greater degree than in our other two states, the various groups act independently. . . . (2) The emergence of conflicting elements beyond merely the teacher's union *within* the education lobby, coupled with broader political conflicts in the state's political system, some of which are between the two major parties, creates a problem for the majority of the education interest groups.[17]

Michigan formerly had a state-wide monolithic structure of educational interests. The Masters data suggested that before 1959 a power structure, capable of keeping educational issues from becoming controversial, did indeed exist, consisting mainly of the NEA.[18] Hence, the state-wide monolithic pattern would seem to devolve into a state-wide fragmented

---

[13] *Ibid.*, p. 73.

[14] *Ibid.*, pp. 92–102, especially pp. 99–100.

[15] *Ibid.*, pp. 36–38.

[16] Nicholas A. Masters et al., *State Politics and the Public Schools* (New York: Alfred A. Knopf, 1964), p. 180. (Author's italics).

[17] *Ibid.*, pp. 105–106.

[18] *Ibid.*, p. 205.

structure. Cooptation, the politics of the priesthood, is replaced by competition, the politics of the market-place. The latter is visible and thrives on the resolution of conflict; the former, hidden and shrouded in mysteries, subsists on the development of consensus. This "revolution" in a state's politics of education would also seem to be coupled with major change in the macrocosm of the state's political system not uniquely involving education.

The syndical structure of Illinois is reported precisely as the result of fatigue and deadlock over educational issues in the state. The deadlock seems to have been the result of the competitive life style of the fragmented mode and the necessary condition for producing the syndical form. Masters *et al.* pointed out that one result of the "go-it-alone" policy, which preceded the creation of the School Problems Commission, was a "perpetual stream of interests pressing the General Assembly for action." [19] Their report indicated that the legislature created the Illinois SPC as a result of Governor Adelai Stevenson's initiative because it was "anxious to find solutions for the many problems in education it faced and to avoid the constant harassment that would result from failure to meet its obligations to the public schools." [20]

A similar sense of frustration by members of the organized profession was noted; one interviewee, representing the Illinois Education Association, said: "Developing a program of school policy which was acceptable to everyone was almost impossible. Every group had its own plan." [21] In other words, before the SPC, Illinois was organizationally fragmented by state-wide associations, which competed with one another in the market-place of public power and displayed no single leadership clique. One might describe Michigan in similar terms after 1959.

The Developmental Construct

In terms of states changing from one type of educational politics to another, the taxonomy offered above can be considered as a developmental construct. The four types of structure would then be phases in the development of political structures for influencing the state legislation of education. However, if the hypothesized system relationships should survive phenomenological testing, it would still be a long way from useful prediction. Even if we could assume survival from such testing, it is necessary to determine what forces, other than the preceding structural mode, are necessary to produce the shift from phase one to phase two, from two to three, and from three to four. The Bailey and Masters reports provide some clues.

---

[19] *Ibid.*, p. 106.
[20] *Ibid.*, p. 112.
[21] *Ibid.*, p. 106.

The major concern of both studies was to describe the politics of education at that time. The task was not concerned, except incidentally, with the genesis or history of the patterns they found. Nevertheless, the studies provide useful contrast.

In addition to the preceding pattern, one factor seems to emerge in states moving from one phase to another: a political realignment, not of education in particular, but of the state's elected power structure. The Missouri study noted this realignment in its present state-wide monolithic phase:

> The MSTA [Missouri State Teachers Association], largely by adopting a strategy of accommodation, has "routinized" the decision-making process. In this way it has been able to gain and hold a predominant or elitist position within the state's political structure. Although the MSTA through its relations with the official agencies of government provides for Missouri a stable and seemingly durable power structure, forces are emerging that suggest this arrangement or pattern is not permanent. . . . Elements of discontent with the low conflict style of politics are increasingly evident. . . . Growing demands for state services from many sources threaten to open the state's politics to much more conflict than in the past.[22]

The study further concluded that the educationists' traditional reliance on political strategies, which are based on values or attitudes of how educational issues should be decided, will become a liability, particularly "when the parties divide on issues that directly affect the schools." [23] The action of the governor and the General Assembly of Illinois produced the SPC! In Michigan, the party division over education and the realignment of political power structures, involving the two legislative houses and the executive branch, seem to have made the Michigan Education Association's old political formula bankrupt. This suggests that a state's change phase in the politics of education is a reconstitution of the state's political system itself.

In judging the probable future of the educational politics in a given state, it is necessary to determine (1) which of the four phases of structure, life style, and leadership best describe that state, and (2) whether or not the particular state is moving from one phase to another. With the political revolution now underway in education, especially as it coincides with reapportionment, chances are that within the next few years more than the usual number of states will undergo a transition from their present phase of political structure. From this point of view, the term "revolution" is a gross overstatement. We would not expect the effects of federal funding, reapportionment, or other forces identified earlier, to be different in kind, only in magnitude, from those effects already noted as a state changes phases in its politics of education.

---

[22] Masters, pp. 97–98.
[23] *Ibid.*, p. 259.

California's case offers additional evidence concerning the utility of the typology described above, as well as the conclusion that new structures, life styles, and leadership groups in given states are likely to follow this pattern. Several studies recently completed in California use the developmental construct of this chapter, in the following ways: (1) to describe the state's educational politics historically; (2) to ascertain that an apparent phase-two to phase-three shift—from a state-wide monolithic to a state-wide fragmented type—did, indeed, demonstrate the change in interest-group structure, political life style, and leadership predicted by the theory; and, if so, (3) to judge whether the changes in pedagogical politics were independent of the state's political macrocosm.

In a study of the relationships between the California Legislature and the education profession, Deane Wiley analyzed published sources and found that the profession was characterized by a locally-based disparate structure between 1849 and 1919. After 1919, with the California Teachers Association as its central agency, the profession, controlled by an oligarchy of school superintendents, perfected its monolithic structure, operating with a predominantly cooptational and conflict-avoiding life style. Thus, for instance, from 1929 to 1962, all of the successfully-elected California superintendents of public instruction ran as incumbents! The high-water mark of this monolithic structure occurred between 1945 and 1952; Wiley described the structure at that time as the "politics of consensus."[24] In contrast, Dean Bowles described California's structure as the "politics of conflict" from 1961 to 1966. His data consisted largely of interviews with participants in the events of each period, as well as one year's participation in the California Legislature during 1965-1966. Bowles documented the phase-two to phase-three shift in greater depth and detail than Wiley had.[25] The failure of the once-monolithic structure to prevent hostile legislation and to control the elected state superintendency after 1962 is directly related to its present fragmented, competitive, and polyarchic structure. These studies documented the development of California's educational politics through three periods which display the sequence indicated by the developmental construct, derived from the study of the reports on eleven other states. In California, at least, the structural sequence from locally-based disparate to state-wide monolithic and finally to fragmented units holds true; the related sequence of political life styles and types of leadership groups also hold.

The relationship of California's changes in the political macrocosm of

[24] Deane Wiley, "Political Interaction of Education and the California Legislature, 1849-1963" (Unpublished doctoral dissertation, Claremont Graduate School, 1966).

[25] B. Dean Bowles, "Educational Pressure Groups and the Legislative Process in California, 1945-1966" (Unpublished doctoral dissertation, Claremont Graduate School, 1966).

the state is also supported by the Bowles and Wiley studies. Even clearer evidence of this issue exists in Lawrence Fahey's work on the California Legislature and the changes in its decision-making patterns between 1957 and 1965.[26] Fahey had spent two and a half years as a staff member deeply involved in the decision-making process of the California Legislature before undertaking his study. His work indicated that the phase-two to phase-three shift (documented by the Bowles study) of the educational interest groups—the fragmentation of the educationist monolith—took place hand-in-hand with a major political change of the legislature. These involved, in part, an increasingly partisan-voting pattern with respect to education (as well as other matters) and centralization of decision-making *inside* the legislature and in the leadership of the lower house. In fact, Fahey observed that the political reorganization of the legislature produced the fragmentation documented by Bowles:

> By 1961 the political revolution of 1958, which had resulted in the Democrats gaining massive control of the executive and legislative branches, had ensnared the educational structure in its turbulent wake. . . . The educational groups could not or would not adjust to the totally different political environment. . . . Confronted with a new political environment, the powerful educational structure fragmented. Although the segments were individually well organized, they were forced to deal with the legislature as multiple units rather than as an organized whole.[27]

Fahey's work was based on his experience in the legislature and on interviews. Both the Fahey and the Bowles studies relied heavily on the reports and the perceptions and observations of interviewees. More reliable from a technical standpoint, although not as significant in producing theory, are the findings of a study on California legislators' voting behavior during the transition from phase two to phase three. Donald N. McIsaac, Jr. tested the hypothesis that a basic shift in the composition of clusters of legislators, as determined by their voting behavior, would be found if the hypothesized transition to fragmentation (since documented in studies of the educational interest group structure) were related to political changes in the legislature itself.[28] He used factor analysis to identify the voting groups in the first, middle, and last third of each of three legislatures. Comparisons of the factors revealed a shift away from groups of legislators displaying geographic and social similarity in their home districts, toward strict partisan clusters.

Speaking of Michigan, Masters *et al.* said, "When the *parties divide* on issues that directly affect schools, the education interests tend to lose

---

[26] Lawrence J. Fahey, "The California Legislature and Educational Decision-Making" (Unpublished doctoral dissertation, Clarement Graduate School, 1966).

[27] *Ibid.*, p. 218.

[28] Donald N. McIsaac Jr., "Statistical Analysis of California Legislature Voting Blocs" (Unpublished doctoral dissertation, The Clarement Graduate School, 1966).

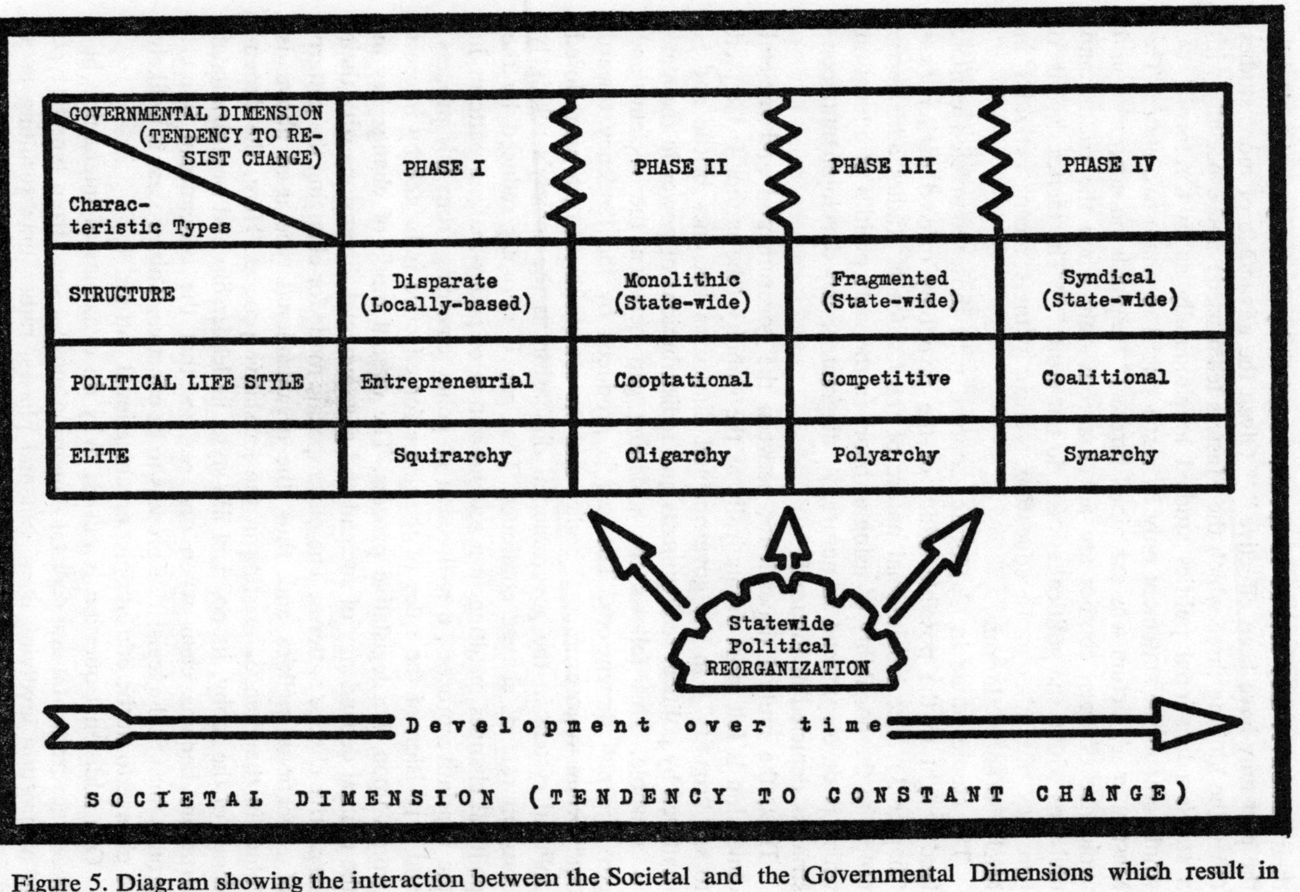

Figure 5. Diagram showing the interaction between the Societal and the Governmental Dimensions which result in changes in the State Politics of Education.

their initiative; they are, so to speak, boxed in by the very tactics that in the past may have been effective." [29] Given the advantage of more studies (than the limiting three which the Masters team used) and especially with a state's educational politics studied longitudinally as in California, we would amend the statement only by restricting it to phase-two states. The Masters *et al.* dictum was explained further: "Emphasis on consensus and avoidance of open conflict are advantageous only when the strains and divisions within the political system do not erupt." [30] The tactics described here are not inherent to education groups; witness recent activities in Michigan and California.

The studies done in California, coupled with those completed earlier, lend weight to the possible utility of the taxonomy offered earlier (*see* Chapter 3). The longitudinal nature of the California studies adds more weight to the possibility of using a theory in the state politics of education which is developmental in nature. A diagram of the developmental construct is depicted in Figure 5.

Thus, the mutual dependence between the governmental and societal dimension is felt most dramatically as the stability (the author is tempted to say "rigidity") in the governmental dimension becomes brittle and is shattered by political realignments and redistributions of power in the state as a whole. This follows the widening gap between the societal and governmental dimensions. The gap is produced by the tendency toward equilibrium in governmental bodies and the establishment of a near-closed political system in the governmental dimension as the society's relatively constant rate of change continues. That gap is abruptly reduced by the political changes resulting in a reorganization of policy-making patterns in the legislative process, a redirection of policy emerging from this process, and a revision of the rules of the game for effective influence by interest groups upon that legislative process. The overall mode of change lies in the mutual dependency of societal and governmental dimensions with their respective change patterns. The more specific mode for changing the pattern of educational politics and, thus, the organizational type used above, is found in the changes existing in the legislative process. Here, the dependency of the lobby, its political life style, its leadership and organizational structure become clear when one realizes that the educational interest groups must fit the legislative process to be effective. This process is unlikely to change to fit the educationist organizational pattern.

One additional question is raised: Why do dynamics of interaction between governmental and societal dimension move a state from type to type in a direction involving developmental phases, rather than resulting in a simple alternation pattern of monopolistic and competitive power struc-

[29] Masters *et al.,* p. 259.
[30] *Ibid.,* p. 18.

tures? Ralph Kimbrough's research (structured on Gladys Kammerer's work on city managers) suggested that *alternation* takes place at the local governmental levels.[31] Without entering a judgment on the local level, two things should be pointed out:

(1) Some elements of alternation are implicit in the four phases. The first phase is competitive among geographic components; the second, monopolistic on a state-wide basis; the third, competitive on state-wide components of differing educational interests; and the fourth tends to be monopolistic, though governmentally regulated. Thus, a gross view would suggest the alternation hypothesis is borne out at the state level of educational politics as well as at the local level, following Kammerer and Kimbrough. It is a finer, more detailed examination which results in a distinction between the organizational nature with its correlates of leadership and political life style of each monopolistic and competitive system. This finer shade of distinction looms large at the state level and may be present at the local level where it is more difficult to observe. Thus, the Kammerer and Kimbrough research on city power structures may have located the gross alternation pattern without identifying systematic sequential variations within the pattern of alternation. Robert A. Dahl's historical review of the New Haven power structures seems to lend support to this hypothesis.[32]

(2) A second factor which may help explain the sequence and show why each phase is different from a simple alternation of competitive and monopolistic power systems lies in a point made by George Homans.[33] He noted that elaborate social structures that continue as vestigial remnants, which no longer function to reflect the requirements of a new social world, tend to become reduced or eroded. But, he pointed out, the process of reduction of social structures is never so complete that it atomizes men's social relationships to the single individual. The primary groups of a social structure remain. Indeed, the process continues until the component fragments of the former system are once again functional. Those elements of an old social system, which can effectively operate in and after a revolution, will survive, whether that revolution is a great national one or a petty political reorganization within a state. Such elements as those found in the state politics of education will be recombined into an organizational structure. Partly through trial and error, the new structure is found to be effective at influencing educational legislation in the new legislative process.

This is illustrated in California's shift from phase two to phase three. The old united front of the one-time monolith, led by school administrators

---

[31] Ralph B. Kimbrough, *Political Power and Educational Decision-Making* (Chicago: Rand McNally & Company, 1964), p. 106.

[32] Robert A. Dahl, *Who Governs?* (New Haven: Yale University Press, 1961).

[33] George C. Homans, *The Human Group* (New York: Harcourt, Brace & World, Inc., 1950), pp. 456–459.

and the California Teachers Association chief officers, has shattered. But its component organizations, such as the California Association of School Administrators and the California School Boards Association, have not ceased to exist. The former relationships among these one-time components of a by-gone informal power pyramid have largely been destroyed. The former components, however, are in many cases more vital, stronger, and more representative of their particular members than they were individually before the phase change. The past carries a heavy residue through the present into the future. Already, there is evidence that the California Teachers Association is having greater effect upon the legislative process than in the immediate past, although it is not as powerful as it was a decade ago. Such victories have been won, however, at the expense of falling-out with the state superintendent's office, and also disaffiliating with the school boards and the organizations of school administrators. Internally, signs of shifting power relations among CTA's regional components and leadership cliques may be seen. These and related changes will move even more rapidly in the next few years, if CTA is to be effective in the phase-three, fragmented, competitive, and polyarchic politics of California's education. It is almost certain that CTA will survive, and what is more, adjust to the politics of fragmentation. It will not become the center of the monolithic interest group pyramid in this phase, holding a monopoly of information to dominate the California legislative process in education; however, it will become even more effective than it was when it had the power to push through a teacher negotiation bill against the opposition of both school boards and the teacher union.[34]

The movement from phase to phase in the changing pattern of state educational politics displays elements of alternation between monopolistic and competitive power systems. This is, however, an all-encompassing view, valuable only as far as it goes. Carrying it further, one may see that residuals, specifically organizational components of a preceding political phase, extend into the succeeding phase of a state's politics of education. These residual components must adjust and reorganize internally; almost inevitably incumbents holding seats of power at the top of these transitional units must be replaced by new men with new habits of political behavior. The relationships among former component organizations must also change. Since each sequential phase carries much of what was built in the past, each successive phase in the state politics of education is significantly different—not only from the phase which immediately preceded it, but also from the one which preceded that.

The construct proposed above is developmental in nature. American

[34] Lee O. Odle, "The California Teachers Association: An Appraisal of Organizational Behavior" (Unpublished doctoral dissertation, The Claremont Graduate School, 1967).

educational policy-making patterns at the state governmental level do change. They change, lawfully and predictably, within the present constitutional arrangements; so, to an extent, changes can be induced, if this is what the American public wishes. A revision of some of the statutory and constitutional special arrangements for education in many states may hasten changes where this is desired. But the constitutional arrangement of education as a state function need not be abandoned, *if the goal is to make education responsive to the society's expressed will.*

CHAPTER 5

Change and Local District Politics

Increasing criticism has been leveled at the local school district and the "myth" of local control. James B. Conant, for example, asserted that the American local school district has proven itself incapable of solving the educational problems of our day.[1] This may be. It is unfair, however, to offer the fact that the local district has not solved the problems of segregation and church-state relations as evidence for this conclusion. To accept such evidence assumes that local voters *in their particular school districts* have wished to apply the preferred solutions of Mr. Conant and similar critics to these problems and that they have failed in the attempt.

Instead, the evidence we have argues in favor of the political viability and responsiveness of the local district. In the face of major financial incentives and threats, despite judicial condemnation, and confronted by hostile officers in the United States Office of Education, local districts continue to express their constituents' desires repeatedly. Thus, the arguments of Conant and others against local control ought to be made openly rather than covertly on the basis of their value choices, not on grounds of effectiveness of the local district system at expressing *its* citizens' wishes. The evidence suggests that these critics disagree with the value choices made by the American voter when he acts as a citizen of his local school district. They may, therefore, take the position that the greater good of the total American society outweighs the value of the local franchise in school matters. However, such value choices are not the product of scientific testing and rest ultimately on belief rather than on evidence.

To assert that the local school district cannot cope with key problems in education is a different matter with supporting evidence. This chapter brings existing evidence to bear on the issue of the *political viability* of the local school district. Does the district reflect the wishes of its constituents? This question does not involve the issue of whether it is *desirable* to allow local citizens the power they have traditionally held over education. Often when the issue of the political viability of the local district is raised in the context of desegregation and church-state relationship, a partly hidden assumption is present—an assumption that the states (severally or jointly in some education compact) or the federal Office of Education have solved these problems. What evidence does, in fact, exist for this assumption? Even the

[1] James B. Conant, *Shaping Educational Policy* (New York: McGraw-Hill Book Company, 1964).

Illinois School Problems Commission, a unique, legally-organized coalition of forces in a state's politics of education, avoids grasping these nettles of social conflict.[2]

Indeed, these knotty problems *provoke* so much heated conflict and pervade American life so completely that they can be resolved only by the central agencies of American government itself—if they can be resolved by government action at all! Neither segregation nor church-state relations is uniquely a public school issue. To say that the local school district is not a viable governmental vehicle because it has not been able to cope with problems which have defied solution by other government units is to close the debate unfairly before discussion. If, instead, it can be demonstrated that local school district citizens not only *can* but by voting *have,* in fact, changed the policy-making machinery and educational policies of their school districts to fit their aspirations for the schooling of their children, then it must be admitted that the local school district form of government is evidently responsive to *local public will.* Such a verdict does not imply that local school districts are as responsive to *local social needs* as they may become. The author believes that all political systems in education are too closed. Despite the closed-system tendency common to educational politics, if the local district displays an identifiable pattern of responsiveness to social change through its school district politics, then an alternative to the centralization of educational decision making at the federal level is available and should be considered. The recent trend has been to dismiss this alternative, rather than to weigh it against the others proposed.

This chapter is finally concerned with evidence about the political viability of the local school district. Specifically, it will focus upon the political aspects of change in educational policy making at the school board level, which is the policy level most open by law to the district's voters. It will also examine the relationship between the school board and the superintendent's office. This discussion will offer a theoretical system consisting of a chain of causation linking the relatively constant rate of social change, which is characteristic of the societal dimension, to the intermittent change, which is characteristic of the governmental dimension.

The Theoretical Backdrop

Thomas Eliot, in his preface to *State Politics and the Public Schools,* asserted that, "There are tens of thousands of districts and in each, the political pattern is different." [3] They are, in some detail or other, and so is

[2] Nicholas A. Masters, Robert H. Salisbury, and Thomas H. Eliot, *State Politics and the Public Schools* (New York: Alfred A. Knopf, 1964) pp. 114–117.

[3] Masters *et al.,* p. v.

every other political unit, sub-system, body, or office. From the point of view of theory, if one is not caught up with minute irrelevancies one can move in his thinking to a level of abstraction and, using the commonalities displayed by these thousands of school districts, see a general pattern of politics. Appropriate adjustments can then be made in the application of general rules to particular instances. One cannot go along with Eliot's further conclusion: "To formulate and test a general theory of school district politics would demand the examination of an impracticably large number of districts." [4]

Instead, the venture summarized in this chapter began with a single case study done in 1961 and 1962 by Frank Lutz at Washington University.[5] It culminated in several verificational studies conducted at the Claremont Graduate School, completed in June, 1966.

Lutz's report, the chief influence on the theoretical development, is a case study of the Robertsdale School Board election which involved the defeat of an incumbent board member by a newcomer to that suburban community. While the defeat of a single incumbent would appear to have little effect upon the leadership of the board or its policies, in this case it did. Robertsdale displayed a shift of board leadership to the new man, culminating in the search for a successor to the superintendent two years before his official retirement! The educational policies of the district underwent major revision, particularly toward improving the communication of teachers and civic groups with the board—in short, opening the policy-making system.

Lutz's study produced a conceptual model for the mobilization of social power within a district to change the board's internal structure of power relationships, its operating procedures, and its program emphases. In itself, the case study is exciting, but it also provides one source of the theoretical backdrop for this chapter.

A second source has been Paul F. Lazarsfeld and others, whose writings offer a picture of voting behavior with respect to the two-party system and provide a limited but valuable theoretical purchase on predicting voter behavior. In essence, this research and discussion in the political party realm has indicated that people tend to conform in their voting behavior to one or the other party.[6] As Gilbert and Sullivan pointed out concerning the British electorate, one is born either a little liberal or a little conservative.[7] Lazarsfeld *et al.* found that small face-to-face groups had the power to shape an individual's interpretation of political speeches, mass media, etc. Thus, small groups, those with whom a person interacts frequently, often

[4] *Ibid.*

[5] Frank W. Lutz, "Social Systems and School Districts" (Unpublished doctoral dissertation at Washington University, St. Louis, Missouri, 1962).

[6] Paul F. Lazarsfeld, Bernard Berelson, and Hazel Goudet, *The Peoples Choice* (New York: Columbia University Press, 1948).

[7] W. S. Gilbert and Sir Arthur Sullivan, *Iolanthe,* Act II, Private Willis' song.

reinforce his habitual pattern of political behavior. Hence, those most active as Republicans or Democrats tend to be surrounded by others similarly active. Those who are habitually most politically active are least likely to suffer cross pressures that might pull them in opposite directions or cause them to exhibit switch voting patterns. Even those who are subjected to cross pressures are more likely to sit out the election without voting than to switch their habitual pattern by voting for the other party.

Even with the non-partisan local election pattern customarily found in education, the findings of Lazarsfeld and other students of politics can be applied. It is not a large leap from their generalizations to local school district elections, given the fact that those concerned with education—the professionals and their usual allies such as PTA leaders—constitute an organized pro-school political faction in school districts. For the tendency to vote for one party, we may substitute the tendency to vote for the local education "establishment"; for the other party, the opposition to the local "establishment." Then, following Lazarsfeld, the school districts will generally have a hard core of "yes" votes for incumbents seeking re-election to the board and for referenda proposed to the voters by these boards. There may be a much smaller "no" vote on these candidates and offices.

If the theory of political change of pulling governmental and societal dimensions slowly apart and then putting them abruptly together also holds, then over a period of time school board membership and policies should remain rather static. It would require changes in the district's social and economic composition for the societal and governmental dimensions to drift apart. The hard core "yes" voters, reflecting the past as well as pro-local school establishment values, should then reinforce the board's relatively static condition until the changing society, through political action, upsets the old system. Then the societal and governmental dimensions in education display a sudden convergence through political activities at the local school district level, resulting from population changes rather than changes in the characteristic voting behavior.

The specific political event, identifying convergence or abrupt change in the governmental dimension, would be the defeat of an incumbent school board member who is running for re-election by a non-incumbent. It seems probable that, if changes in a school district's populace were to take place *without* similar changes in the governmental policies, then an election upset would occur disturbing the internal alignment of the board, reshuffling the power distribution between the board and superintendent, and changing the direction of educational policy. If the policies of a school district are largely the product of the district's superintendent of schools, then their destiny becomes his fate. The hypothesized political shift, resulting from incumbent defeat and closing the previously wide gap between societal and governmental dimensions, would place the chief school district's administrator's tenure in danger.

Research on the tenure of city managers seems to point this way, too. Gladys Kammerer and her associates, studying city-manager tenure and turnover in relation to community political change, found specifically that "manager tenure and turnover are positively related to power exchanges." [8] The Kammerer group used a questionnaire study of all the Florida council-manager cities to investigate the phenomenon of involuntary turnover of city managers.[9] In addition, they studied ten of these cities, using intensive interviewing. They began with the realization that, however non-political the city managership might appear in the folklore of public administration, the traditional line between politics and administration could not be clearly drawn. The role of the city manager, like the role of the superintendent of schools, as it becomes caught up with policy making, cannot avoid becoming political in nature. The presence or absence of *partisan* politics does not change this.

Kammerer and her group found that city managers "tend to play major policy roles in the making of the principal decisions of the city, and, therefore, they tend to incur political hazards," [10] and they found that managers were heavily involved in policy making and, therefore, deeply enmeshed in politics. Thus, managers inevitably alienated certain interests in the city, making themselves the target of political action. The Kammerer team also found that tenure was longer for city managers in politically stable cities. Thus, in their data, where the political control of the city council shifted from one group to another, the non-political (*sic*) city manager services were likely to be terminated involuntarily. "Power exchanges" existed behind the political changes in the councils where one leadership clique replaced another in controlling community government. Furthermore, behind these "power exchanges" were changes in the societal dimension. Changes of population, particularly migration into a community, were most likely to be reflected in the pattern of power exchanges, shifting control of the council and involuntary termination of city managers:

> What is crucial is that, in some cities, the newcomers do not share the interests of the old guard, and that the sons of the old guardsmen do not always share the clique policy orientations of their fathers.[11]

This seems equally true in school districts where incumbent school board members are defeated.

---

[8] Gladys M. Kammerer, Charles D. Ferris, John M. DeGrove and Alfred B. Clubok, *City Managers in Politics* (Gainesville: University of Florida Press, 1962).

[9] Gladys M. Kammerer, Charles D. Ferris, John M. DeGrove and Alfred B. Clubok, *The Urban Political Community* (Boston: Houghton Mifflin Co., 1963), pp. 206–210.

[10] Kammerer *et al., The Urban Political Community,* p. 192–193.

[11] Kammerer *et al., City Managers in Politics,* p. 73.

Students of community power structures have usually noted the relationship between the power structure and the school board. Floyd Hunter noted that school board members were second-line power figures; the top-line group entrusted the board to lesser figures who were dependent upon the top group for status.[12] In studies of smaller communities, such as the research of Vidich and Bensman, the school board has been more closely related to the core of the power structure.[13] Daniel E. Griffiths wrote that generally the members of the school board are either power-holders or representatives of power-holders.[14] Finally, Lutz pointed out:

> The school board is a group which reflects a portion of the social structure of the total school district and provides a point of tangency between the formal school organization and other elements of the social structure of the school district.[15]

The controlling power group in a given community will reflect the dominant interests, aspirations, and values of that community. So long as they continue to reflect these factors, they can continue, all else being equal, to wield power. As power-holders interested in the community's fundamental goals and direction, they will be interested in who sits on the board of education and what kinds of policy decisions are made by that board. Further evidence of the close relationship between the power structure and the school board has been furnished by Keith Goldhammer, who wrote that the degree to which the board can maintain itself in power is related to:

> (1) The acceptability of candidates to the dominant power structure, (2) the general apathy of the electorate in school board policies, and (3) the strength of the power structure to confront challenges to it.[16]

Therefore, looking at both the superintendent and the board of education, one must conclude that they are enmeshed in the political system of the school district, if not in a partisan (two-party) sense, then in every other sense of the word, and that they are linked to the community's power structure. In time the board with its superintendent will display a tendency toward closed-system politics, stability, and increased boundary maintenance, contributing toward stability and closedness. It will change intermittently and abruptly as a result of unusual political action by the community, reflecting the widening gap between board and public. Changing

---

[12] Floyd Hunter, *Community Power Structure* (Chapel Hill: University of North Carolina Press, 1953).

[13] Arthur J. Vidich and Joseph Bensman, *Small Town in Mass Society* (Garden City, N.Y.: Doubleday & Company, Inc., 1960), pp. 174–201.

[14] Daniel E. Griffiths, *Human Relations in School Administration* (New York: Appleton-Century-Crafts, Inc., 1956), pp. 95–119.

[15] Frank W. Lutz, "Social Systems and School Districts" (Unpublished doctoral dissertation, Washington University, 1962), pp. 7–8.

[16] Keith Goldhammer, "The Administration of the Community's Schools," *American School Board Journal,* 139 (October, 1959), p. 28.

socio-economic conditions within a given school district will lead to changing expectations for many aspects of community life, especially the schools. Given the general rules of voting behavior, as in the two-party pattern, it may be expected that most often new forces, *not switching votes,* will produce political change. Should the new forces become large enough and well enough organized in a school district to challenge the incumbent power structure, severe conflict is inevitable. It is improbable that a community group, holding power on a school board through incumbents, will give way to their opponents without a struggle. The evidence of the conflict will be the struggle for office, the contest for seats, and the control of policies. For many years the same people, or their representatives, may easily win election and re-election with little or no opposition in a school district. When competing power structures exist, the situation is far different; then candidates debate issues and challenge policies. The schools themselves come under attack. Incumbents may be defeated, or they may be victorious in a strongly contested election. These are the signs of community conflict and struggle for dominance over the power structure, and thus for control of the decision-making processes. If the old power clique fails to retain its control, then there will be a shift on the board of education.

What does this imply in terms of superintendent tenure? People involved in policy determination are necessarily subject not only to having their policies opposed and even repudiated, but also to removal from their decision-making positions by one form of political action or another. The board of education is quite obviously subject to removal, but it is hypothesized that the chief school officer is similarly vulnerable. School superintendents, frequently considered non-political, are necessarily involved in politics because of their participation in policy determination for their communities. As such, their positions, like those of the city managers in the Kammerer study, will be attacked when a change in the power structure of the community brings a new political orientation to the school board. Thus:

(1) Changing socio-economic conditions within a given community will lead to changes in the values, aspirations, and interests of the society encompassed by that community.
(2) Changes in values, aspirations, and interests will tend to give rise to competition for control of the decision-making processes of the community in order to bring them into closer alignment with the new value orientations of the community.
(3) Should the newer interests embrace a sufficient number of the body politic to make an impact on the formal and informal power centers of the community, conflict will result as groups compete for control of the power structure.
(4) The school board, as one of the important formal policy-determining bodies of the community, will be one of the focal points of the conflict;

competition for seats on the board will result in frequent changes in board memberships as different groups alternate in control of the board.

(5) The chief school officer, as a policy maker, plays a political role with all that this implies; therefore, his tenure will be affected as alternate power cliques gain control of the school board.

The Claremont Studies

A number of studies were undertaken at the Claremont Graduate School to test the effect of the defeat of an incumbent school board member and clarify its meaning. According to the foregoing discussion, one would expect the turnover of superintendents to be significantly greater following school board elections in which incumbents were defeated, than following elections in which no incumbents were unseated. Incumbent defeat might also be described as "involuntary turnover" on the school board. Therefore, if incumbent defeat signifies rejection of the current policy-making system, and if it is equally valid that the chief school officer is a strong part of that system, then it follows that involuntary turnover in the board of education will be followed by involuntary turnover in the office of superintendent.

On the assumption that the governing board of the school district would reflect the power structure of the school district and that a change in the power structure would be reflected in a change in the composition of the school board—a "change in composition" being defined as the defeat for re-election of one or more incumbent board members—*the first hypothesis* was:

> A change in the composition of the school board will result in a change in the occupant of the chief school office within three years, except where the chief school officer is within four years of retirement or where he has been employed as superintendent for three or fewer years.[17]

The second hypothesis was:

> When turnover occurs in the office of the superintendent, involuntary turnover will be significantly higher when there has been a change in the composition of the school board within the previous three years than when the board has not undergone change during that period.[18]

All school districts in four Southern California counties which had five-member school boards and which had not undergone any boundary changes between 1956 and 1965 were selected for the study. The study encompassed one hundred seventeen school districts where (a) school board members were elected by direct vote of the people and (b) superintendents were appointed to their offices by their respective school boards.

Data were gathered on all school board elections and board membership

[17] John C. Walden, "School Board Changes and Involuntary Superintendent Turnover" (Unpublished Doctoral Dissertation, The Claremont Graduate School, 1966), pp. 26–27.

[18] Walden, p. 27.

changes for the period of the study. All changes in the office of superintendent were recorded and a questionnaire was employed to determine the nature of turnover in each instance. After the initial analyses, interviews were used to examine all cases which apparently deviated from the hypothesis.

Briefly, election data for each school district from the election in the spring of 1956 through the election of 1963, subjected to chi square (x^2), supported the prediction that the incidence of superintendent turnover would be greater after defeat of an incumbent than after no defeat. This turnover took place within three years of the incumbent defeat.[19]

The questionnaire also asked respondents to judge the stability of the politics of their school district. The election data gave a strong presumption of instability at the point when an incumbent defeat took place. If the questionnaire responses had disagreed with the voting evidence, one might doubt the questionnaire results; however, they went together. The key question had been used, moreover, to find out whether the respondents were perceptive, because the question of involuntary turnover rested, in part, on the assumption that the respondents *"knew" and would report as they knew*. The questionnaire respondents were two kinds of superintendents: one, where incumbent defeat had preceded the turnover of a superintendent; the other, where prior incumbent defeat had not taken place. These were statistically tested with regard to the question of political conflict. The facts of voting behavior agreed with the questionnaire responses involving eighty-seven superintendencies at the .001 level of significance.

The data further suggested that incumbent defeat is not only related to the political stability of the school district, but is also a reflection of a struggle for power between an incumbent power group and an emergent one. To this key question a strong majority of the respondents indicated that the political instability of the school district was the result of "major controversies" within the community. Only a few suggested that personality clashes were the major factor. This factor looms large for the author, indeed, larger than the numerical responses or proportions involved, although these are a heavy majority of the responses. Having worked with school superintendents for years, we are startled to hear of *any* turnover or community struggle over educational matters treated as *anything but personalities!* This is one of the protective administrator myths: "It's not my policies they don't like; it is only a personality clash." Therefore, when a close examination of the data indicates that major controversies rather than personality issues characterize the political instability of the school district at the point of incumbent defeat, it is clear that policy and differences of value orientations in the district underlie incumbent defeat.

---

[19] Walden, p. 79.

Such defeats are most often a result of a shift of school district power structures and may function usefully as an indicator of this. Eighty-eight of the ninety-one questionnaires returned answered the question of superintendent voluntary–involuntary turnover. Again the data supported the hypotheses.[20] The information about the nature of superintendent turnover subsequent to the defeat of an incumbent board member clarifies the situation: not only are superintendents "turned-over" more often after incumbent defeat, but also, while it is not public knowledge, their departure tends to be *involuntary:* they are eased out of the job.

In summarizing, where school district politics were relatively stable, with few controversial questions causing divisions among the people of the district, school board members suffered few defeats and superintendent turnover, when it occured, was voluntary. In contrast, where political instability was evident, school board incumbents were defeated and superintendent turnover occurred more frequently and was usually involuntary in nature. The role that politics plays in the superintendent's life is clear. His tenure in office is closely linked to the results of school board elections. In a sense, as John C. Walden has pointed out:

> Those who aspire to the superintendency must realize that they will play the political game and their fortunes may rise and fall just as do the careers of other political figures whose judgments must meet the challenge of the political market-place. . . . Schoolmen must understand that in a very real sense, at each school board election there is a silent candidate whose name does not appear on the ballot. It is the superintendent of schools.[21]

Finally and most dramatically, the defeat of only a *single* incumbent school board member was necessary for superintendent turnover, for better turnout, and for predictions to be borne out. It was not necessary for a majority of the board to be changed, or for even two board members to be changed. In the case of five-man boards, the one who defeated an incumbent carried a community mandate, as the other board members realized within three years at least. Exceptions exist,[22] but they are few and far between.

Less clear but no less meaningful is the role the superintendent plays in local school district politics. Walden went beyond the test of his hypothesis to examine deviate cases, which did not conform to the hypothesis. In the process, some of the characteristic forms of exceptions which prove the rule were found. More important for the question of political role played by superintendents, it was the superintendent as *de facto,* although not *de jure,* leader of the board who fought the newly elected board member (the one who replaced an incumbent member of the superintendent's team). In

---

[20] Walden, pp. 89–96.
[21] Walden, p. 157.
[22] Walden, pp. 103–144.

the few cases where the superintendent's team on the board and *his* local education power structure won, Walden had found an exception to his central hypothesis. Incumbent defeat there was not followed by superintendent turnover because the defeated incumbent was not of the superintendent's group. Thus it was in the Lutz study, and in the Jefferson School District. The superintendent played the political role of *de facto* leader of the board.[23] In the last case cited, at least, the superintendent also played a political role with regard to the selection of nominees for the school board election. Superintendent Donnelly of Jefferson was routinely consulted and had an effect upon the *selection of nominees* by the non-political (*sic*), non-partisan, nominating committee of lay citizens in Jefferson.

Recently, Roald Campbell, Luvern Cunningham and Roderick McPhee pointed out the increased concern in the literature for caucus committees, formal and informal.[24] The number of these committees is on the increase. This is not surprising. One gap produced by the special arrangements for governing education and the elimination of the two-party system at the local level is *nomination*. The power to nominate is usually more important than the power to elect. One can predict that the blue-ribbon nominating committee system, the caucus pattern, wherever it is found, whether the formal result of law or informal, will be heavily influenced by the local professionals.

In general, one would expect regular progressions through the PTA, Citizens Advisory Committee, and other school-directed associational networks, to provide the regular path to school board nomination by the caucus and then membership. Where this is so, the superintendent will often influence the nominations, as Donnelly in Jefferson. The incumbents defeated by new men are most often picked after consultation with the superintendents. It is therefore probable that the defeated incumbents are not only part of a board team led by the superintendent but are also, in part, selected by him. They are his team. Hence, the new man, having defeated the superintendent's team member, is frequently confronted by the superintendent, very often unexpectedly and bewilderingly *at first*. If he learns quickly, and if he does represent a genuine shift in the relationship between governmental and societal dimensions, then as his bewilderment ends so does the superintendent's tenure of office. The superintendent is complex; he plays more than one political role. Not only does he influence nominations, he is also the board's team leader, identifying educational needs for its members, influencing decision making, and guiding policy that

---

[23] Laurence Iannaccone, "The Social System of a School Staff" (Unpublished Doctoral Dissertation, Teachers College, Columbia University, 1958).

[24] Roald F. Campbell, Luvern L. Cunningham and Roderick F. McPhee, *The Organization and Control of American Schools* (Columbus, Ohio: Charles E. Merrill Books, Inc., 1965), pp. 167–170.

emanates from it. If he miscalculates the future by leading a conflict against the new man on the board, who can blame him? His men are under fire; his policies under attack. Having led the old troops to defeat, the superintendent should not be surprised when his moving day comes.

However clear the political role of the superintendent and the role of politics in his life may be, two essential questions must be answered before one can be sure that the relationships found between incumbent defeat and superintendent turnover do signify the convergence of *changing* societal and *stable* governmental dimensions. Even though the superintendent turnover subsequent to incumbent defeat is involuntary in nature, a relatively meaningless series of palace revolutions might account for the data found. Also, evidence of conflict between the old superintendent and new board member would be enough to explain turnover. What evidence is there that *changes* in the societal dimension account for incumbent defeat? What evidence argues that the replacement of one superintendent with another is intended to have any effect on policy in education? The answers to these are crucial to an evaluation of the issue: *How viable is the local school district system?*

The implications, which the data on involuntary turnover hold for change, lead us in two directions: the Walden questionnaire data, cited above, and the succession pattern in the cases involved. As the author pointed out,[25] the evidence elicited from respondents, themselves successor superintendents, indicates that policy issues divided the boards and separated their predecessors from the districts and offices involved. There is stronger evidence in the succession pattern itself. Before discussing these data, a fourth and final theoretical strand must be woven into the Claremont studies from *Executive Succession and Organizational Change: Place-Bound and Career-Bound Superintendents of Schools,* by Richard O. Carlson.[26]

Carlson reported the difference between insiders and outsiders coming into the superintendency: (1) the insiders were appointed to the superintendent's office after a career of employment *within that same district;* (2) the outsiders sought the superintendency outside their present districts. As Carlson stated, "Ultimately two courses of action are open to the would-be superintendent: one is to wait until the superintendency comes to him, and the other is to seek a superintendency wherever it can be found"; [27] hence, his terminology, "place-bound" for the insider and "career-bound" for the outsider. In summarizing the differences between these two types of superintendents, Carlson included the following elements:

---

[25] Walden, pp. 85–88.

[26] Richard O. Carlson, *Executive Succession and Organizational Change* (Chicago, Ill.: Mid-West Administration Center, University of Chicago, 1962).

[27] Carlson, p. 7.

> School boards elect insiders to the superintendency only when the judgment has been made that the schools are being properly administrated. . . . School boards give outsiders, but not insiders, a mandate to act in regard to organizational development and the necessary support. . . . [Regarding his first generalization, Carlson said:] The conditions of employment indicate that school boards will be satisfied if the insider keeps things as they are, but they expect and are satisfied with an outsider only when some changes are made. School boards hope for creative performance from outsiders and are happy with a stabilizing performance from insiders.[28]

The mandate given to outsiders is equally clear and significant; the outside man is expected to change matters:

> In a very real sense the outsider is given a mandate from the school board. The discussions preliminary to election are devoted to a give-and-take between the outsider and the board. Problems are worked out. The board makes it clear that *all is not well* and there is some interest in righting the situation. There is usually no specification of what needs to be done, but what is specified is what is wrong, what the central problems are. By inference and by word, the outsider is given a mandate to act with respect to the problems.[29]

In other words, the choice of an insider is a choice for maintaining the status quo and a vote of confidence in the immediate past. The choice of an outsider may have no implications for change when it results from a lack of qualified insiders.[30] Most of the time the decision to turn to an outsider is an indication of change, not only of the person of the superintendent, but also of his educational policies, directions, and of the particular school organization. Clearly, the selection of an outside superintendent will usually result in more change than the selection of an insider.[31] Equally clear in Carlson's cases and in the experience of consultants to school boards looking for outside men, the decision to look for an outside man usually indicates that the board feels its problems can be solved better by an outsider. In short, the search for an outsider is most often an indicator of a felt need for change in the school district. It is a search for a change agent.

This line of reasoning led to Robert M. Freeborn's contribution to the Claremont studies. Freeborn, using the work of Carlson and Lutz, offered the following hypotheses:

> The selection of a new school board will lead to or be followed by the selection of a new superintendent, within three years, who will be an outside man. . . . The continuance of an old school board will result in a continuance of an old superintendent. When an old board is faced with

---

[28] Carlson, pp. 69–70 and p. 18.
[29] Carlson, p. 20.
[30] Carlson, p. 18.
[31] Carlson, pp. 23–60.

the selection of a new superintendent, it will choose from within the organization.[32]

Freeborn's definitions were a modification of Carlson's terms, "insider" and "outsider," but did not depart from Carlson's concept of an outsider being a "stranger" to the district.

Freeborn used all five-member board school districts in three Southern California counties, one hundred seventeen in all. With Walden, he studied roughtly a decade of their political history involving six hundred ninety-two elections. One hundred twenty-one instances of superintendent turnover were found between 1956 and 1966, which, in turn, were related to the defeat of the incumbent board member and agreed with the reported strong relationship between turnover and incumbent defeat.[33] The prediction was supported that outside superintendents would be appointed by boards where incumbent defeat had taken place within three years of that political change, and inside men would be appointed where incumbent defeat had not taken place. Freeborn found a significance level better than .001 supporting this hypothesis.

The school districts, displaying incumbent school board member defeat, produced a significantly higher amount of superintendent turnover. The nature of this turnover was more often involuntary than not. Political struggle in the community was, indeed, present while these events took place. Incumbent defeat results in the importation of a putative "change-agent" superintendent, not accidently, but deliberately. It is possible that the involved boards do not know *what* has to be done—this may require professional expertise—but that they want change is clear.

Freeborn's restatement of his hypotheses, after analyzing his data and his deviate cases, is noteworthy. Some deviate cases had involved instances of bringing in outside men without a preceding defeat of a school board incumbent; whereas, some insiders came into office after incumbent defeat. Examination of his deviate cases resulted in the following statements:

(1) The selection of a new school board will result in a power struggle on the board and will lead to or be followed by the selection of a new superintendent who will be an outside man. (This will normally be accomplished within three years.)

(2) The continuance of an old school board will result in a stable board condition and a continuance in office of the old superintendent. When an old board is faced with the selection of a new superintendent, it will choose from within the organization.

(3) Where the selection of a new board does not result in a power

[32] Robert M. Freeborn, "School Board Change and The Succession Pattern of Superintendents" (Unpublished doctoral dissertation, The Claremont Graduate School, 1966), p. 17.

[33] Freeborn, p. 152.

struggle on the board, and the subsequent selection of a new superintendent, it will be found that the effect of the new board removes an anti-administration board member or continues a change pattern already underway (including following the appointment of a new superintendent within three years).[34]

Freeborn concludes:

> The defeat of a single board member is a powerful indicator of a feeling for a need for organized change . . . a signal that some change is wanted. . . . There appear to be indications that other indicators, besides an election defeat, may represent a feeling for a need of change. The possibility that three, or even two, board incumbents retiring concurrently serves as such an indicator is suggested by an analysis of such cases.[35]

Richard Kirkendall was concerned with exploring the possible indicators and signs *preceding* incumbent school board member defeats. Essentially he operated on the notion that change in the societal dimension would be seen first in social and economic circumstances and then in political activity leading, by stages, to the incumbent defeat pattern. His question outlined his task:

> Can indicators of social, economic and political conditions in school district communities be used to discriminate between those school districts in which change in the composition of the school board occurs and those in which it does not occur?[36]

If indicators are found which discriminate between the two kinds of school districts, questions of time become important. One relates to the chronological order in which these indicators appear; the other, to their relative position in time with respect to board incumbent defeat in the change districts. Specifically, the two secondary questions are stated as follows:

> In cases in which indicators of social, economic and political conditions in school district communities discriminate between those districts in which a change in the composition of the school board occurs and those in which it does not occur, do the social and economic indicators precede in time the political indicators?
>
> Can some indicators of social, economic and political conditions in school district communities be used to predict later change or non-change in the composition of the school board?[37]

To answer these questions, Kirkendall used a subsample of thirty-six districts from the one hundred seventeen used by Freeborn and Walden.

---

[34] *Ibid.*

[35] Freeborn, p. 155.

[36] Richard S. Kirkendall, "Discriminating Social, Economic and Political Characteristics of Changing Versus Stable Policy Making Systems in School Districts" (Unpublished Doctoral dissertation, The Claremont Graduate School, 1966), p. 15.

[37] Kirkendall, p. 16.

Eighteen of the thirty-six had experienced incumbent defeat; the others had not. Using discriminant analysis, he found ten indicators which completely distinguished the eighteen districts having incumbent defeats from the eighteen not experiencing incumbent defeat. His findings were statistically significant at the .0005 level.[38] Moreover, the cluster of variables producing this distinction was a mixture of six socio-economic indicators and four political variables. Finally, the point in time when the discriminating socio-economic variables were identified preceded by several years the point in the district's history when the political variables were taken. In short, Kirkendall's study provided strong support for the belief that changes in the societal dimension lead to political activities which result in the abrupt shift in the governmental dimension following the defeat of an incumbent board member. Thus, a process is set into motion which results finally in the selection of a putative change-agent successor superintendent for the district.

The two variables Kirkendall found that contributed most powerfully to the discrimination were:

> (1) Percentage change in assessed valuation over the three year period, 1951-52 to 1954-55.
>
> (2) Ratio of votes against incumbents to total votes cast in the 1959 board elections.[39]

His incumbent defeat cases all took place in 1961 elections. Assessed valuation, one of the most frequently used indicators of social class, changed most sharply *seven to ten years before* the political upset of incumbent defeat. The political indicator which stood out strongest (and was, next to assessed valuation, the strongest contributor of the ten variables) was evidence of changed voting behavior in the election immediately preceding incumbent defeat—but not yet strong enough, not yet consolidated enough, to defeat an incumbent. Thus, two necessary causes which combine for incumbent defeat are: (1) changes in the social class composition of the particular district followed some seven to ten years later by (2) political action to upset the district's status quo. As Kirkendall stated:

> The best discriminations between change and no change communities are made when socio-economic and political indicators are used together. In fact, very poor discrimination is made when either group of indicators is used alone. . . . Change in socio-economic conditions is a necessary but not sufficient cause for a change in the formal power of a community.[40]

The questions raised earlier may now be answered. The data involving all one hundred seventeen school districts over a decade suggest that, while

---

[38] Kirkendall, pp. 65–91.
[39] Kirkendall, pp. 104–105.
[40] *Ibid.*

the boards of school districts, chosen and led in part by established superintendents, continue the policies of the past, the school districts themselves undergo changes in social class composition. Although this is a gradual process, it has peak moments. When one of these peaks is followed a few years later with an unusual rise in votes for non-incumbents, the stage is set for an abrupt shift in the district's power structure as it converges upon the board. Thus, it is probable that a group of newcomers to the district, representing a social-class shift and, hence, least likely to merge easily into the existing power structure, are central to the incumbent defeat pattern. Equally important is the probable rigidity of the old team on the board and the team leader, the superintendent of schools. The defeat of an incumbent is apparently achieved by a consolidation of opposition forces during the period between the election which has a large anti-incumbent vote and the next election which replaces an incumbent. The defeat of the incumbent leads to conflict on the board, especially between the new member or members and the superintendent. Usually within three years, he is eased out of office. His replacement is an outsider with a mandate to change the schools. At the local district level, the intermittent-change pattern of the governmental dimension and the relatively constant-change pattern of the societal dimension move along a collision course toward incumbent defeat, involuntary superintendent turnover, and the selection of an outside superintendent.

This pattern, first found at the local level in case studies and then tested with verificational studies, confirms the capacity of local school districts to change themselves or their schools. The operation of even relatively blind forces follows social laws. In the case of the local school district, these do produce change, bringing a school into alignment with its society. The application of intelligence through eliminating legal barriers which hinder this pattern of change in particular states may be wise. Efforts to institutionalize a loyal opposition in school districts may speed up the process. Knowledge and better understanding of the process itself should result from helping the foundations which are concerned with educational change to better equip themselves to select the educational changes (not to mention the federal programs). Better training of boards and superintendents can produce awareness of these patterns and use of the early indicators to adjust educational programs to the needs and aspirations of their citizens. In no way do the findings of these studies justify the conclusion that the local district "must go" because it cannot or does not change educationally to meet its citizens' demands!

CHAPTER 6

The Future

Few generalizations concerning human behavior, individual or group, have stood the test of time as well as, "Past behavior is the best predictor of future behavior." It would be foolhardy, indeed, if one were not to ask, "How different will the new day be?" As suggested earlier, politics and education have been and are inextricably tied to one another; this will be true until education has no impact on the political beliefs and behavior of a society's young, or the adult leaders of a society do not find in education the vehicle for shaping the values and social commitments of their children. Even beyond the yellow brick road, Dorothy and her companions needed green glasses to "see" the Emerald City in the Land of Oz.

Any group (set of organizations or confederation of co-professionals) will engage in boundary maintenance to stabilize their internal distributions of power, and will tend to develop a closed social system with closed cooptational politics as their preference, if the society allows it. Educationists are prone to cooptational politics because the behavior characteristic of effective teaching requires persuasion above all else. Hence, the preferred pattern of pledagogical politics, cooptational in nature, fits the requisite occupational skills.

Earlier than any other major public service in America, education acquired special legal protections against the operations of "normal" politics. The almost complete elimination of overt linkage to the party political mainstream of British and American democracy has functioned to facilitate the closed-system politics of the priestcraft as practiced by pedagogues. This has given schoolmen a better opportunity to control their universe, compensating for the legal vulnerability of local control, especially in obtaining local school district financial resources. As the state's portion of financial support has increased, the legal protections, special arrangements, and the "insider's edge" in the educational world have produced closed political systems reinforced by the emotional appeal of motherhood, suffering little children, and spinster schoolmarms. The result, particularly in urban education, has been nearly disastrous. Little innovation takes place at any level in education.

The evidence seems clear that, given the opportunity, educationists will play out their preferred political style. It is the politics of the priestcraft rather than the politics of the marketplace, consensus building rather than conflict resolution, the dull etiquette of gossip rather than the sparkle of debate and verbal exchanges of the hustings. Cooptational manipulation characterizes the internal power struggles of the education association, too. Again, closing the educational operations of the urban centers follows the customary pattern and aggravates the large city's already-grave problems. The changes in education required by the society further depend for their fulfillment upon the shifting power relationships of the macro-political systems of state and local district rather than the leadership of educationists. Major political power must always be brought to bear for basic reform to take place, whether the issue is school district reorganization, reform of the state certification laws, or the local school curriculum. This, briefly, is the price paid for the lack of a *loyal internal* opposition.

Political systems are never closed. Consequently, educational reform does come and with it change in policy and decision-making patterns. Reform seems to come too slowly, too irregularly, and too painfully, but, contrary to the statements of many critics of local control, it does come. The fact that it takes political action by community leaders and sections of the public not adequately represented under existing arrangements only underscores the close-system tendencies built into the government of education and reinforced by traditional educationists. It does not argue that educational policies and practices cannot be changed even under present arrangements, for they frequently are.

Similarly, and particularly in California's case, educational reform may take place *as one result of political reorganization of the legislature and the state*. However difficult this may seem, the fact that educational policy-making change takes place at both state and local levels of government conflicts with the argument that the present governmental mixture of state and local district cannot change education. It is clear that major changes in the governing of education at state and local levels of government do systematically occur. Since this is true, it may even improve the existing pattern of government response to society's wishes. At least, there is an alternative to nationalizing education, if people want one.

Factors already apparent indicate that changes will take place slowly by trial and error. Furthermore, changes from one phase to another at the state level will occur with increasing frequency. New forces (or old ones revitalized) are beginning to play a part in the political arenas of education, suggesting a development of loyal opposition within the educationist world. Despite the delay imposed by the resistance of the professionals to educational innovation (educationist myths to the contrary notwithstanding), one must suspect that the public does get the educational changes it wants for itself and its children.

New Forces

Several new and some old but reawakened forces are becoming significant in educational policy making. These are making new alliances, bedfellows, combinations and coalitions of political actors; e.g., the political right wing and a state superintendent of education in California, a teachers' union and school board association in New York opposing supervisors. Among these new forces, several deserve mention before attempting to discuss the future of educational politics, for some will have an impact upon that future. These include: ideological groups, the foundations, the new federal education officials, groups of professors who have at last considered public schools worthy of notice, teacher organizations with a new-found militancy, and businesses whose research units have recently discovered gold in what had been considered ivory towers.

Groups with an ideological base somewhat different from the national majority have always seen an opportunity for their growth in education. From book-burning in Scarsdale to the Pasadena story, the early 1950's saw struggles over ideological issues which sometimes ended with a superintendent moving out, but more often with broad community support for schoolmen. More often than not attempts by extremist groups to take over boards and school districts have failed when they were exposed, forced into the public arena, and openly debated. The politics of minorities traditionally provided advantages to schoolmen. This brand of politics, however, allows other minorities to take advantage of the small proportion of voters necessary to control a school district, such as the recently strengthened right wing. The near future will witness an increase of political activity by minorities not controlled by schoolmen.

Quite different, and contributing to a changing political future, is the interest and concern for public education exhibited by college professors and American intellectuals since World War II. In the latter half of the nineteenth century the public school expansion, as a result of the universal high school, let the burden of teacher training fall upon normal schools and teachers colleges. Until recently, schools of education have made money for private universities and helped produce friendly legislatures for public universities. Both kinds of schools, following one form of the adage of not letting the right hand know what the left was doing, served their universities and liberal arts colleges by ignoring quality in the interest of quantity. As a result, there was until recently "a warm body" called *teacher* in every public school class room, and the professors in the humanities, science, and social science disciplines could wash their hands of responsibility for them.

More recently, the intellectual community has displayed a different interest in teacher training. Fortunately, this renewed interest in the schooling of children by the academicians and the intellectual community is being reinforced by the fashion of the day, by the technical revolution requiring as true a universal education as possible, and by a beginning of resources from private foundations and the federal treasury. It is not surprising that some educationists view with cynical smiles the new-found concern with public schools by the professors in fields which once considered school teaching an occupation for the harmless but not-too-bright rejects from their departments. This cynical view is unfortunate because other factors beyond the increasing financial support for academicians interested in education have also influenced this concern in public schooling. Whatever the motivation, educationists are finding it necessary to take this group into account in policy making.

The efforts of foundations to influence education have been related in several different ways to the academic community's interest. Some foundations have operated in public schooling as one might expect *parvenus* to any field would. A majority of their money for schooling went into immediate action projects; therefore, they would prefer not to evaluate their work. But such haste is to be expected. It is the price one almost always pays to learn how to make a real difference in any area. This short-sighted immediacy also characterizes recent federal government programs. It would be more useful to view the 1960s' waste of federal funds in education as a continuation of the foundation pattern exported from New York City to Washington, D.C.

One problem with these weaknesses is that very little solid research on schooling exists. Consequently, paradoxical though it may seem, it *is easier* to throw monies around on trial and error projects for early starting or late blooming pupils, and for dropout students or drop-in teacher aides. Were a more solid knowledge of schooling available, the random use of resources would be less. As regrettable as the waste is, one has learned it is the hallmark of the twentieth century affluent society and possibly a necessary phase on the road to using real resources in schooling. The point is that men such as John Gardner, former president of the Carnegie Corporation; James Conant, supported by that corporation; and Professor Lawrence Cremin, sometime distinguished educationist consultant to Conant, are performing a valuable function in shaking up the old systems.

If what the foundations have produced by way of educational innovation seems trivial, it is understandable. Often, those who lead out of the past find it impossible to build the future. We are all imprisoned in the concepts we learned. Reformers conceive of themselves as the obstetricians of the future while history declares them the morticians of the past. The process of change influenced by the public policy making of the foundations, and even more recently by the "foundationeers" in government, must be endured. One would wistfully hope that enough of the resources, otherwise going down the "demonstration" drain, could be used for careful evaluation and decently descriptive research so that there would be a chance of knowing *why* something does work and *repeating it* when it is successful. In any case, the injection of tempting packages for school districts and federal grants for "different" programs constitute a new element in the superintendent's political life.

One effect of the federal spending program in education warrants mention because of its ironic and almost poetic justice. State departments in education have not provided aggressive leadership of creative intellectual contributions to the solution of educational problems. Too often, they seem to have functioned as a political appendage of the state's educationist interest-group elite. Recently a number of these departments have discovered that their respective urban centers have educational problems. The stimulus for this discovery has been the possibility that the city's schools would by-pass their state departments and work directly with Washington, D.C., on poverty and other programs, thus "tapping the federal till" without going through their state departments. The old treaty by which the rural-based and biased state pyramids of educational interests and the autonomous city school with its own private deals and closed-political system—that old treaty has become a clear and present liability for state departments. Awareness of this will eventually open the city. (For now, however, such federal funds going into the city schools are being used to prop up the existing pattern.) Here, too, in the relationship of the United States Office of Education with the urban schools, one finds the beginning of a new and powerful interest in the state and local politics of education.

The last of the factors changing the politics of education is the rising militancy of organized teacher groups. This has its ironic touch, too. It exists, in part, as a result of the internal closed-system power plays of educational associations and in part as a consequence of improvements made by the profession in teacher training. More often, however, it exists as a product of the economic facts of the affluent society, itself largely the fruit of twentieth century schooling. Since World World II, the United States has experienced chronic crisis conditions of teacher shortage. There have generally been "warm bodies" at teachers' desks in every classroom each September, but often little more. This condition reflects the pressure of population and public awareness of the value of schooling as well as the job opportunities competing for college-trained young people. Those who have come into and remained within teaching are sometimes a bit more competent and well-trained than the critics of education may believe; some have even read about the history of labor in America! Others seems to have taken the title, *Goodbye, Mr. Chips,* too literally for the peace of mind of school board members and school administrators, with the result that some teachers, particularly men in the cities, seem as bold as other professionals.

This combination is producing an organized teacher militancy both inside and outside the National Education Association. The long-run trend of this is unsure, but one of its effects is appearing now. School administrators are finding it increasingly difficult to operate on both sides of the desk. The united front of educationists at the state level of government becomes more and more difficult to maintain, especially with school board and teacher associations attempting to get together. This rising teacher militancy may be the most critical factor, leading to a new political world in education.

Finally, an actor appearing in a new role with new interests at stake is the businessman. The sale of textbooks and their profits led to purchasing scandals in the 1920s. Equipment suppliers and contractors for school buildings have had the same motivations, opportunities, and temptations to get into the political selection and "influence game" in school districts as in any other form of government. Publishers contributed heavily to the campaign in a recent election for superintendents of schools in a state where the state department influences the selection of text books. But a new element of interest has been injected into the situation as industry acknowledges the gross American expenditure in education and as public criticism of education turns to that great American dream, "I can get it for you wholesale." A new salesman's heaven exists in panacea mechanisms, which range from specially-programmed computer labortories to modified mimeographs labeled "teaching machines," not to mention sophisticated audio-taped equipment for teaching foreign languages (in some instances gathering dust because the local pressure is off and because, "It didn't cost anything; it came from the government"), or complete television operations (some actively in use and some gathering dust through the courtesy of the Fund for the Advancement of Education).

Even newer are the corporations or sub-units of larger corporations engaged in the business of research. These public problem-solvers, engaged, for a price, in purifying the gamut of ills ranging from poverty to pollution, have become the "wheelers and dealers" of educational research—sometimes "pseudo research." Some of these operate as tax-free "growth" combinations which are acquiring power almost as great as the economic stake they already have in the continued, unchecked, and expanded federal funding of applied educational research projects. Such corporations are finding out: (1) there is money in the "Ed Biz"; (2) nobody trusts schools or even universities to do research on public problems as much as they trust industry; (3) industrial research outfits can get large education contracts from the government faster than schools or colleges can; (4) research groups hire educationists from colleges, universities, or school districts to supply "expertise" in education, pay them more than they are accustomed to, and no one challenges their expertise. In this way every organized force can be happy so long as national taxpayers, consumers, and pupils remain relatively unorganized. The situation does produce a large lobby interested in increased federal financing of educational fads and changes; the lobby, also, constitutes a significant political influence in and on the future politics of education.

Predictions

Listing the old or new *dramatis personae* on the political scene involving education does not provide a picture of the future. It does suggest that educational politics to come may be far more open than heretofore. If so, its rules and alignment of forces are less predictable than they would otherwise be. The more open a social system is, the less predictable it is, and the less useful is past behavior as a predictor. The amount of knowledge unused in the educational process is the most limiting factor on the future. We know much less about a child's schooling than we do about an albino rat's maze learning. The new world of education will offer, for some years to come at least, a faster-paced series of fads consisting of nineteenth century teaching techniques (and teachers) with twentieth century packages labeled "twenty-first century education."

Far more important to the next decade for the politics of education than federal funding, in the author's opinion, is the effects of the *Baker vs. Carr* decision.[1] The "one man, one vote" rule is producing a rapid series of reorganizations of legislatures, realignments of political structures, and redistribution of rural and urban power. The twin facts of increasing organized teacher militancy centering in the cities and the virtually complete reliance on rural structures of the educational interest pyramids in the dominant Type II pattern of educational politics, make more legislative conflicts highly probable. These will produce shifts into Type III. Thus, more fragmentation patterns of educational politics are in the immediate offing. New York and New Jersey should be closely observed for this. The negotiation legislation of Connecticut and Wisconsin suggest these states would also bear watching. Safer is the general prediction that an increase in the number of abrupt shifts in patterns governing education, both state and local, are in the offing. Reapportionment will mean the doldrums of consensus are past for many states. At the same time, an increasing number of incumbent defeats can be predicted for the states moving into open political conflict, since the political microcosm seldom insulates itself well enough from the macrocosm.

A period of stress, a time of political change, an era of social revolution—almost bloodless and petty though it is—offers increased opportunities for planned change. Planning takes intelligence, but intelligence is not enough. One use for human intelligence in social affairs is to provide knowledge,

---

[1] *Baker v. Carr,* ——369 U.S. 186, 82 Sup. Ct. (1962).

understanding, and predictability of how men behave in groups and in public roles. The function of such understanding is to reduce the impact of chance factors on the future. What is needed to avoid some of the waste in the usual political process of change is the application of such understanding (especially by foundations and volunteer citizens' groups interested in education) to pinpoint targets which should use the resources to facilitate change. The federal government may have difficulty because of the "log rolling" traditions in using this selective approach. The foundations and citizens' groups operating with limited resources might better apply these judiciously to the districts and states in transition. There the future is most open, the choice of alternatives real. A state or a district, ready by its own developmental history for change, begs to be helped toward becoming whatever its greater potential allows.

Several research directions need immediate attention. They should be faced directly. A habit, unhealthy for all concerned, has been developing in the small world of educational researchers: it is the habit of bootlegging research into action projects because more monies are available for action, while monies for basic research in education are almost non-existent. This is too bad. Such bootlegging too often produces an ill-tasting brew. Instead, quality research in education is needed too desperately to "slip it in" under another guise.

Three types of research in the politics of education should be undertaken, at once, for effective action programs: (1) The developmental construct of changes in the state politics of education should be tested in additional states. It should, at the same time, be simplified as overlapping categories are merged empirically. Hard data, easier to collect than with the field study techniques, should be one goal of such research leading to verificational studies and the identification of handy indicators for elements in the developmental phases. (2) The chain of causation worked out at the local district level should be made more solid by replication in another part of the country throughout its length, especially at the societal-change level where the present research is partly exploratory. In addition, it should be extended into what the successful new man, the outsider superintendent, does on the job, so that educational change reaching to the pupils actually takes place. The utility of such information does not require discussion. (3) One or more data banks on school districts and change-agent superintendents should be created. This would provide, at the time needed, information on school–community readiness for educational change. With this knowledge, agencies concerned with educational-innovation can specifically channel their resources to facilitate the local district's development at a time when it is ripe for educational change. It would make significant contributions to educational adaptability, resulting in fewer dusty, expensive facilities which "cost nothing because the government gave it."

Bibliography

Bailey, Stephen K. *et al., Schoolmen and Politics.* Syracuse, N.Y.: Syracuse University Press, 1962.

Campbell, Roald F. *et al., The Organization and Control of American Schools.* Columbus, Ohio: Charles E. Merrill Books, Inc., 1965.

Campbell, Roald F. and Bunnell, Robert A., eds., *Nationalizing Influences on Secondary Education.* Ill.: Midwest Administration Center, University of Chicago, 1963.

Carlson, Richard O., *Executive Succession and Organizational Change.* Ill.: Midwest Administration Center, University of Chicago, 1962.

Carter, Richard, *Voters and Their Schools.* Stanford: School of Education, Institute for Communication Research, 1960.

Conant, James B., *Shaping Educational Policy.* New York: McGraw-Hill Book Company, Inc., 1964.

Dahl, Robert A., *Who Governs?* New Haven: Yale University Press, 1961.

Freeman, J. Leiper, *The Political Process.* New York: Random House, Inc., 1955.

Griffiths, Daniel E. *et al., Organizing Schools for Effective Education.* Danville, Ill.: Interstate Printers and Publishers, Inc., 1962.

Hunter, Floyd, *Community Power Structure.* Chapel Hill: University of North Carolina Press, 1953.

James, H. Thomas J., ed., *Boardsmanship.* Stanford, California: Stanford University Press, 1961.

Kammerer, Gladys M. *et al., City Managers in Politics.* Gainsville: University of Florida Press, 1962.

Kammerer, Gladys M. *et al., The Urban Political Community.* Boston: Houghton Mifflin Co., 1963.

Kimbrough, Ralph B., *Political Power and Educational Decision-Making.* Chicago: Rand McNally and Co., 1964.

Lazarsfeld, Paul F. *et al., The Peoples Choice.* New York: Columbia University Press, 1948.

Lutz, Frank W. and Azzarelli, Joseph J., *Struggle for Power in Education.* New York: The Center for Applied Research in Education, Inc., 1966.

Martin, Roscoe C., *Government and the Suburban School.* Syracuse, N.Y.: Syracuse University Press, 1962.

Masters, Nicholas A. et al., *State Politics and the Public Schools.* New York: Alfred A. Knopf, 1964.

Munger, Frank J. and Fenno, Richard, *National Politics and Federal Aid to Education.* Syracuse, N.Y.: Syracuse University Press, 1962.

Packard, Vance, *The Pyramid Climbers,* N.Y.: McGraw-Hill Book Company, Inc., 1962.

Sayre, Wallace S. and Kaufman, Herbert, *Governing New York City*. New York: Russell Sage Foundation, 1960.

Usdan, Michael, *The Political Power of Education in New York State*. New York: Institute of Administrative Research, Teachers College, Columbia University, 1963.

Vidich, Arthur J. and Bensman, Joseph, *Small Town in Mass Society*. Garden City, N.Y.: Doubleday and Company, 1960.

Warner, Bloomberg Jr. and Sunshine, Morris, *Suburban Power Structures and Public Education*. Syracuse, N.Y.: Syracuse University Press, 1962.

Index

Index

A

American Association of School Administrators, 24, 30, 31
American Federation of Teachers, 20, 22, 49, 65

B

Bailey, Stephen, 41, 44, 45, 62, 68, 71, 73
Bensman, Joseph and Joseph Vidich, 10, 11, 39, 87, 60
Bowles, Dean, 75, 76
Butler, Nicholas Murray, 20, 23, 24, 46

C

California Association of School Administrators, 80
California Teachers Association, 75, 80
California School Boards Association, 80
Campbell, Roald, 4, 92
Carlson, Richard O., 32, 93, 94
Carnegie, Corporation, 37, 102
Chicago Teachers Federation, 20, 22
Claremont Graduate School Studies, 84, 89, 93, 94
Conant, James, 3, 37, 82, 102
Cunningham, Luvern, 4, 92

E

Eliot, Charles W., 23, 24, 46
Eliot, Thomas, 83
Evans, Seymour, 58

F

Fahey, Lawrence, 76
Freeborn, Robert, 32, 94, 95, 96

G

Gemeinshaft, 50, 51, 58, 60
Gesellschaft, 50, 51, 58, 60
Goldhammer, Keith, 5, 44, 87
Griffiths, Daniel E., 13, 87
Gross, Neal, 5, 6

H

Harris, William T., 20, 23, 25
Homans, George, 12, 79
Hunter, Floyd, 48, 87

I

Iannaccone, Laurence, 3, 10
Illinois School Problems Commission, 49, 53, 73, 74, 83

J

James, H. Thomas, 29, 42
Jenkin, Thomas P., 1, 2

K

Kammerer, Gladys, 31, 79, 86, 88
Keith, Everett, 64, 70

Kimbrough, Ralph, 4, 5, 42, 79
Kirkendall, Richard, 96, 97

L

Lazarsfeld, Paul F., 84
Lutz, Frank W., 84, 87, 94

M

Martin, Roscoe, 4, 5
Masters, Nicholas, 3, 6, 10, 11, 41, 44, 49, 50, 62, 72, 73, 76
McCarty, Donald, 6, 31
McPhee, Roderick, 4, 92
Missouri State Teachers Association, 64, 74
Moeller, Gerald, 60
Mort, Paul, 6, 23, 30, 62, 68–70

N

National Education Association, 19–22, 24, 46, 48, 60, 64, 65, 67, 72
New Hampshire Joint Committee on the Needs of Education, 71
New York City Board of Examiners, 27
New York State Citizen's Committee for the Public Schools, 67
New York Congress of Parents and Teachers, 67
New York State Educational Conference Board, 64, 66, 67, 68

P

Parent Teachers Association, 6, 48, 67
Pearse, Carroll G., 20, 24

S

Schafer, Eldon G., 31, 32, 33, 34, 35
Schmid, Ralph D., 19, 20
Solden, F. Louis, 20, 23

U

United States Office of Education, 82, 103
Usdan, Michael, 41, 44, 62, 68

V

Vidich, Arthur J. and Bensman, Joseph, 10, 11, 39, 60, 87

W

Walden, John C., 91, 95, 96
Wiley, Deane, 75, 76
Wilson, Charles H., 5, 6